The Earl Covey Story

A Master Builder in the Adirondacks

Frances Alden Covey
with
Mary Alden Covey Williams

St. Johnsbury **Athenaeum** Press

Printing History
First Printed 1964 by Exposition Press, New York, NY
Second Printing 2010 by L. Brown & Son, Barre, Vermont

All rights reserved
Copyright 2010 by
Mary Alden Covey Williams

ISBN: 978-0-615-34671-7

All photos are from the Covey and Williams family collections.

Cover, book design and editing by Terry Hoffer

Contents

I	The Early Years	7
II	The Twitchell Years	19
III	A Fresh Start	51
IV	Henry Covey	65
V	Covewood	70
VI	Covey's Polar Grip Tire	95
VII	Big Moose Community Chapel	103
VIII	The Later Years	124
IX	Earl's Failing Health	148
X	Summer 1952	159
	Appendix	167
	Afterward	170

Chapter I

The Early Years

One day in the summer of 1951, Earl Covey asked if I thought he should write the story of his life. While packing and preparing to return north from Florida a year later, I found in his desk two sheets of paper on which he had made a beginning. This is what he wrote:

> Earl Covey was born on the 27th day of November in the year 1876, in the little town of Glenfield, Lewis County, N.Y., coming to Old Forge and the Fulton Chain the summer of 1885 for the first time with his mother. They stayed several weeks at the head of Fourth Lake at the Meeker Camp with the owner, Captain John Meeker, and his family. Later in the season and early fall we stayed for a few weeks at the head of Third Lake with Bobby Ferry, then returning to Glenfield for the winter.
> During that winter Father built a portable camp in Warren Johnson's shop. It was a camp consisting of two good sized rooms, one a living room, the other a bedroom divided with a heavy canvas curtain, a lean-to room on the back, which was used as a kitchen and dining room. This camp was put together with hook and eyes. It was made in panels about four-feet wide of one-half inch spruce with a studding strip 3 x 3, in which was plowed a groove to receive the panel. The plate and shoe was plowed also to receive the panel so that the building was tight and mouse proof. When it was finished Father got a team and brought it to Old Forge on sleighs. The following spring 1886, we came to Old Forge and set the building up at the foot of Fourth Lake on the north side of the channel between Third and Fourth Lake and we spent the summer there,

that is, Mother and us two boys. Father was guiding at that time and was away most of the time. A great deal of his time was spent at Big Moose.

Earl was near the end of his second sheet of paper when the writing stopped. It remained for another time or another sheet to continue where he had left off.

While Earl began his story at the time he first went to the Adirondacks to live, his family had lived in upstate New York since the early 1800's. His paternal grandparents, George [1] and Nancy Covey, came from northwestern Vermont into St. Lawrence County. Later they moved into Lewis County and lived in the town of Croghan. George was a blacksmith by trade. So was his son Henry, the third of George and Nancy's four children. Henry was to be Earl Covey's father.

Earl's mother's family, the Chases, came from England before 1750. An ancestor named William Chase settled in Valley Falls, Rhode Island. Descendants of William settled in Plainfield, Connecticut. In 1802, one of these, Reuben Chase, married Eunice Alexander, daughter of a captain in the Revolutionary War. Some time afterward the young couple moved to New York State. Possessed of considerable energy, Reuben was at various times a lay preacher in the Methodist Church and a mail carrier on the first mail route from Utica to Sacketts Harbor. He was the builder of the first brick store building in Lowville, New York.

The next two generations of the Chase family lived in the town of Watson at Chase Lake, which was named after Reuben's son Charles. Charles, with his eldest son, George Wellington Chase, did carpentry work and operated a small sawmill. They built several homes and a small hotel at Chase Lake. Wellington Chase, "an hon-

---

[1] In 1889 George Covey of Alburg, Vermont, moved into New York State after his barn had been burned by a raiding party from across the Canadian border. Inasmuch as the Vermont records do not give the name of his wife or the place where he settled in New York State, it cannot be definitely established that he and Earl Covey's grandfather were one and the same person. It exists, however, as an interesting possibility.

The Early Years

Henry Covey's young bride was Emma Chase from Chase Lake in Watson about twelve miles east of Lowville, New York.

est, kindly man," married his cousin Martha Chase. They had five children. Their third child, Emma, had "gorgeous red hair," which she wore in thick braids.

In 1871 Leroy Crawford began the manufacture of hemlock extract at Chase Lake. He purchased Chase's sawmill, which he operated along with another mill on Independence Creek a few miles away. He used horses for lumbering and hauling, and to keep them shod he had to have a blacksmith. Henry Covey from Croghan got the job.

Perhaps it was Emma Chase's red hair that first attracted the attention of Crawford's young blacksmith. Henry began to court her. Then he asked her to marry him. She was not yet fourteen.

Miss Anna Crawford, daughter of Leroy, relates the following: "I remember hearing my mother say [Emma's] parents did not want her to marry, but she wept and wailed and cried, 'Do you want me to be an old maid?'"

Emma finally won their reluctant consent, and on January 10, 1874 she and Henry Covey were married. They lived for a time at Chase Lake and then moved to Glenfield. There Henry built a blacksmith shop and went into business for himself. Their son Clarence Covey was born in December 1875, and the younger son, Earl William, was born on November 27, 1876.

Earl's childhood was in most respects like that of any boy living in a small community of that day. He remembered the loss of the tip of his left forefinger, severed by a corn-cutting machine. He maintained that he was only two years old when this occurred.

There was the time when he and his brother, Clarence, sliding downhill, were being teased by some bigger boys. After enduring this for a while Clarence picked up his sled and, holding it by the rope, swung it in the direction of the tormentors. The teasing stopped.

Henry Covey was one of the first to make a permanent home on Big Moose Lake. Known as Camp Crag, his camp became the home for his family and, gradually, a popular hotel attracting a discriminating and affluent clientele. Photo taken about 1922.

There were other, happier memories — the Sunday-school picnics at Brantingham Lake and the taste of his mother's blackberry pickles. Earl kept these early memories with him as long as he lived.

The Coveys lived in Glenfield until Earl was nine years old. Meanwhile Henry Covey acquired property on Big Moose Lake for a summer resort, one that was to become well known for the simple comfort it afforded to those who loved the seclusion and quiet of the woods. The family came to the Adirondacks that summer for the first time. They stayed in Old Forge at first, later moving to Fourth Lake while Henry was busy with his project at Big Moose.

By the summer of 1886 the Coveys had a camp of their own at Third Lake, assembled earlier in Glenfield in the manner described by Earl himself in the beginnings of his autobiography. An old photograph of the camp bears an inscription in Henry Covey's writing: "Our First Home in the Adirondacks." In the picture Henry, Emma, and their elder son, Clarence, are grouped near the front of the cottage. Back in a corner of the porch, sitting by himself as if too shy to have his picture taken with the others, is a small childish figure look-

The Early Years

Henry H. Covey was a builder, trapper, hunting and fishing guide and a popular innkeeper.

ing down at something he is holding in his hands.

The child is Earl. One can see in his face the look of quiet serenity, which was to characterize the mature man years later.

After going to the woods to live, Earl and Clarence obtained their schooling in first one place and then another. For several winters they returned to Glenfield. In 1888 they went to school in Moose River, six miles from McKeever where with their mother they boarded at Charles Barrett's hotel. From there they used a sled drawn by a team of dogs to make occasional trips to Big Moose Lake, where their father was at work building and guiding. The boys later joined Henry at Camp Crag, which from then on became their permanent home.

During his boyhood in the Adirondacks, Earl Covey knew none of the conveniences of modern living. Anyone who ventured to make a life for himself in the woods during those days had to have the capacity for hard work and the courage and resourcefulness of a pioneer. Henry Covey, the son of pioneers — his parents were among the early settlers in upstate New York — was himself a pioneer. He was one of the first to make a permanent home at Big Moose Lake. From his father Earl inherited that venturesome spirit,

Camp Crag promised the purest of spring waters, first class bathing beach and daily mail. In this dining room one found a bountiful table with fresh milk and eggs. Gradually Covey added separate cottages with mesmerizing views over Big Moose Lake.

which manifested itself in a variety of ways throughout his life.

Earl's mother's ancestor, Reuben Chase, was also a pioneer. But Reuben's descendants lacked the ambition and physical stamina characteristic of the Coveys. Several fell victim to tuberculosis. One can surmise that the gentler traits of modesty, kindness and friendliness, which endeared Earl to all who knew him in his later life, came from Earl's mother and her people.

Emma Covey never lived at Camp Crag. Apparently inheriting the family weakness, she too contracted tuberculosis. That made it necessary for her to remain in Old Forge to obtain nursing care, which she could not have received in so remote a spot as Big Moose Lake. For two years, Earl divided his time between the camp and Old Forge, where he helped to take care of his mother. Emma died in 1890. [2.] She was thirty.

For the next year and a half, life at Camp Crag continued as it had begun, with building, guiding, getting in supplies, cooking and housekeeping all done by Henry and the two boys. While Clarence assisted his father as guide on hunting and fishing trips, Earl looked after the camp.

In their spare time the boys provided their own recreation. They tamed two young raccoons, which were a source of much interest and amusement. The dogs were pets and companions, as well as useful animals. The dogs worked the treadmill to pump water, hauled loads and, as was permissible in those days, were used for hunting deer. Fishing, bathing and boating helped to compensate for a hard and at times a lonely life.

On August 21 in 1892 the fun turned to tragedy. The boys were out in a canoe made of a pine log off Turtle Point. [3] Clarence moved to one side of the canoe. It tipped, and he fell into the water and sank instantly. When he did not come to the surface, three shots from Earl's gun brought Henry Covey to the scene. Henry came quickly, but he was too late to save the boy from drowning. This was the second time in two years sorrow had come to the Camp Crag family. A monument in the family lot in the Beeches Bridge Cemetery in Watson, New York marks the final resting place of Emma Covey and her elder son.

During her last illness Emma had as nurse a young woman by the name of Margaret Rose. About a year and a half after Emma's death, Henry Covey married again. His second wife was that nurse. Margaret proved to be a good wife and mother as well as a hard worker. To relieve the dogs when their feet became sore, she and Earl would work the treadmill to keep the pump in operation.

One of the first contacts Earl had with the Rose family was the winter he attended school with the children of John Rose at Moose River. It was the beginning of a lifelong friendship between Earl and John's son Tom, who was in Earl's own words, "like a brother." By

---

[2] Henry Covey, builder of the first hotel on Big Moose Lake, and Jim Higby, who built the second hotel on the Lake were friends from childhood. They were hunters and trappers together and Adirondack guides. They even married sisters, Ella Chase (Higby) and Emma Chase (Covey). Both women died of tuberculosis leaving the old friends as widowers to raise their sons.

[3] Later known as Retter Point.

After Emma's death in 1890, Henry married Margaret Rose, a nurse. Photo, taken in 1892, shows (L-R) Clarence, Henry, Margaret and Earl Covey.

1892 the Roses moved to Jayville, a small upstate mining community, where John was made a school trustee. In this capacity he obtained the services of Miss Helen McGarry, his children's former teacher in Moose River. Thus it came about that after Clarence's death, Earl, instead of returning to Glenfield for the winter, joined the Rose family in Jayville to attend school there. Miss McGarry therefore knew him as a pupil in both the Moose River and Jayville

The Early Years

schools. While in Jayville Miss McGarry boarded with the Rose family.[4] As a member of that household she knew Earl in the home as well as in school.

The schoolhouse was a frame building heated by a big woodstove in the center of the one room. There were sixty pupils ranging from the first grade to beginning high school. Earl, a very good student, was in the highest class.

"Besides being a good student Earl had very good habits and was a very likable boy and well thought of by his classmates," was the tribute paid him by his teacher. She recalled further: "The boys at that time stayed at home nights, and after they did their homework, they would play games or sing. Mr. Rose had a wonderful voice and we would all sing Gospel hymns."

That winter, when Earl was sixteen years old, was probably his last in school. The Jayville iron mine had been abandoned, people were leaving the community, and the school was discontinued after that year.

From then on Earl helped at camp, building and guiding. He knew what it meant to be alone. On one occasion in his father's absence he was for days the only person on all of Big Moose Lake.

Once however, when he had been left in camp, some guests arrived unexpectedly and wanted a guide. Earl packed their supplies, took them out, acted as guide and cook and brought them back with more to show for their trip than had the guests who went with his father. For his services Earl received $128. For a long time afterward, Henry Covey took delight in relating his son's successful experience with this party.

Although Earl's school days were over, he and Tom Rose continued to keep in touch with each other. For several summers when Tom was at Camp Crag, the two boys worked together. To Tom, Earl was "a good friend" with "a sense of honor."

Even those early years at Crag were not all work. There were picnic parties with some of the girls who worked there. One of Tom's special friends was a waitress by the name of Addie Butts.

---

[4] A few years later Helen McGarry married James Hall of Oswegatchie, New York.

Earl Covey and Addie (Butts) were married in 1895. The wedding was at Addie's home in Scriba, New York north of Syracuse on Lake Ontario. This photo, taken about 1899, includes Earl and Addie with their children at the time, Emma and William.

The Early Years

When Tom later became more interested in someone else, Earl invited Addie to go with him on a picnic. It was not long before their friendship ripened into romance, and in February, 1895, Earl and Addie were married at Addie's home in Scriba, New York. After the wedding they left for a honeymoon in Washington, D.C.

Their trip proved to be more than a honeymoon. The Coveys decided to stay. Earl obtained work on a contract to furnish railroad ties for a short line between Washington and Georgetown, eventually becoming foreman on the job. One can only speculate what Earl Covey's life might have been had he remained in Washington. His integrity, his skill, his amazing capacity for hard work, combined with a friendly, winsome personality would have won him recognition in whatever he might have undertaken.

He had already made a good start during that year in Washington when word came from New York that Henry Covey needed help at Camp Crag. Could Earl return to do some work for him?

Would Earl give up the prospect of a successful career in the nation's capital with a family to support? His son born in Washington was then a few months old. Going back to the hard and primitive life of the Adirondacks of that day was perhaps the most difficult decision Earl ever had to make. But in response to his father's request he returned with his wife and young son to Big Moose for the summer and fall of 1896. They occupied a cottage not far from the entrance to North Bay.

The Coveys spent the winter of 1896-97 in Scriba, where Emma, their second child, was born. When they returned to Big Moose Lake the next summer Earl helped his father with building for which he was paid ten dollars a month. As a guide Earl could earn three dollars a day, with an additional dollar a day for his board. The second winter after their return from Washington, Earl and his family remained at Big Moose Lake. In order to earn money through the winter he did some trapping on lakes and streams in the area. When making the rounds of his traps he would take a dog with him, stay out overnight and cover a distance of some thirty miles.

He had already earned a reputation for honesty, for his willingness to do hard work and for his being "so nice with his family."

With his energy and initiative, and with a family dependent on him, Earl was not content to rely on guiding and trapping as a means of livelihood. Whether he ever had thoughts of returning to Washington we do not know, but one thing was certain. He did not want to work for someone else. He wanted to be independent. His father thought that he should purchase property and remain on Big Moose Lake, but Earl decided that one Covey on the lake was enough. Before the end of 1898 he bought land near the southwest end of Twitchell Lake, with a view to having a place of his own.

After seeing Addie and the children settled in Scriba for the winter, Earl and his helper George Matheson went back to Twitchell, where they spent their first night, February 19, 1899, in a spot hollowed out from a snowbank. The next morning the two men began work on what was to be the Twitchell Lake Inn.

Chapter II

The Twitchell Years

When Earl began building the Twitchell Lake Inn he had no sawmill. For the half-logs on the main house he used a pit-saw. Two planks, placed far enough apart to permit the blade of a saw to move between them, were mounted on supports about a man's height from the ground. A long, two-man saw extended vertically through the platform made by the horizontal planks. The log to be sawed was laid on the platform. One man stood on the platform, the other on the ground below. Each grasped a handle, and they sawed up and down through the length of the log. In this way Earl did his first rustic work at Twitchell, sawing it out by hand.

Half-logs were lined on the inside with waterproof paper, spruce battens covering the logs where they joined. The ceilings were of whole logs peeled and flattened on the upper sides to take the boards for the floors of the rooms above. There were three rooms downstairs, a kitchen, living room and dining room. Upstairs were seven bedrooms, two for the family and five for guests.

When Earl Covey began work on the Twitchell Lake Inn he did so without a sawmill. Instead the long logs were ripped with a pit saw. One man stood on the platform, the other on the ground below.

During the cold winter months the family lived in the kitchen with a stove large enough to take wood three feet long, it was the warmest room in the house. A drum in the upper hall, which was connected to the stovepipe from the kitchen, helped to take the chill off the bedrooms. From the time the children were small Earl made a practice of getting in a winter's supply of apples, which he stored in the unheated cellar. At night the children took apples with them when it was time to go upstairs to bed and placed them over the holes in the drum to warm them. Sometimes the heat from the drum partly cooked the apples before they were eaten.

It was not long before the need for a larger dining room and more sleeping rooms became apparent. Lacking the ready money for material, Earl went to Camp Crag one day to ask his father for a loan. Not in a lending mood, Henry Covey told Earl to get the money in a way that he, Earl, would know how he came by it.

Earl returned home, changed his clothes and left for Herkimer on the midnight train to see William Taber, an official in one of the banks in that community. On hearing Earl's story, Mr. Taber lent the money on a personal note without asking for additional security. Earl purchased the material he needed, and as soon as it was possible he paid back this loan.

The Old Road

At the time of Earl's midnight trip to Herkimer, the only way he could reach the Station was over a trail so rough that supplies for the Inn had to be loaded into a pack-basket and carried on one's back. Loads too great to be thus "packed in" were carried by a "jumper," a

The Twitchell Years

The first crossing of the Twitchell Lake outlet was simple but suited to loads carried in back packs. Most supplies and guests were taken to the end of the Lake and then by boat to the Inn. Gradually the trail was improved as a corduroy road allowing the use of horses and buckboards.

sled-like conveyance built on runners of stout timber. These runners had to be replaced frequently, so great was the wear to which the rough trail subjected them. During spring thaws the mud was knee-deep. When Earl built Balsam Cottage he ordered spruce ceiling for finishing the interior. When it arrived at Big Moose, he kept it clean and out of the mud by carrying the material to the Inn on his back. It took several trips to get it all there, but it reached the Inn without being spattered.

Later the trail was improved somewhat by the building of a corduroy [1.] road, which permitted the use of horses and buckboard. [2.]

Even then there were rocks in the way as high as the hubs of the wagon wheels. Some found it easier to walk than ride. Sometimes on the hill approaching the first bridge on the way to Twitchell it was difficult to control one's speed; the wagon would get going so fast that when the brake was applied sparks flew from the metal rims of

[1.] Logs laid crosswise on the road and packed with earth.
[2.] A carriage having no springs.

the wheels.

One of Earl's guests at that time tells of a trip he made over the road: "We started out in a wagon for the lake. We had a good-sized trunk, which I tried to sit on, but I had to give it up after a short distance and walk. I shall never forget how that wonderful team (Chub and Jerry) just sat down and literally slid down Twitchell Creek hill."

This guest had a particular fondness for Earl's team of horses. He continues:

> I remember Earl telling about the time one of the old team of Chub and Jerry broke through the ice. Of course he couldn't climb out as the ice kept breaking. And so Earl put a chain around his neck and choked him until he floated up. They dragged him out, took him ashore and poured a quart of whiskey down his throat. He must have felt better for some time.
>
> And what a wonderfully trained team they were. Earl used to let me drive them. But really all you had to do was talk to them in the language they had learned. That winter old Jerry dropped dead on the way in from the Station over that terrible road. We went down the next morning with Chub to drag the poor old fellow out of the road and bury him. I think old Chub realized he had lost his partner, for the last quarter mile he kept up a constant whinnying. It certainly gave me a lump in my throat as I thought a lot of that team of horses. Old Chub died soon afterward, I am sure of a broken heart.

The horses may not have been young to begin with, and it is more than possible that the poor road shortened their lives.

There are other stories of the old road. Someone provided the following account: "All guests arriving at Big Moose donned heavy walking shoes for the walk in over the rough road. Children too young to walk were carried in pack-baskets. It was not unusual to see several men starting off after the arrival of a train, each with a child in a basket (on his back) and a suitcase in each hand. On one occasion Earl, besides a suit case in each hand, carried a pack-basket containing a five-gallon can of milk, on top of which was a crate of berries."

The Twitchell Years

With a vision of a place to call his own Earl Covey bought land at the southwest end of Twitchell Lake before the end of 1898. The following February he began what was to become The Twitchell Lake Inn. This photograph, dated 1899, shows the Inn in its earliest form. Several later modifications included an addition to the right, second floor balconies and an elaborate stone entrance replacing the wooden stairs seen above.

Another time when the road was in such condition that no vehicle could be taken over it, a horse was loaded with one pack of supplies while Earl, shouldered the other. At the Inn when both packs were weighed Earl's was found to be the heavier of the two. In the early days before there was a bridge across Twitchell Outlet the guests, their luggage and all supplies had to be taken to the end of the lake and from there by boat to the Inn. Of all the stories about the old road, the following is a favorite with the Coveys:

> The old road was so rough it was almost impossible to stay on a lumber wagon or to keep anything on it, and so most of the supplies were drawn in on what was called a "jumper," a sort of sleigh

with very heavy runners of green birch or beech with natural crook at the front so it would slide over the rocks along the road. Planks were used for the bottom of the jumper with sideboards of planks and stout beech stakes to keep the groceries and other supplies from falling off.

On one occasion the teamster bringing in a load lost a ten-gallon can of milk on the way. After unloading the rest of the things he went back to look for the milk. It was so deep in the mud, the top was barely visible, but he managed to pull it out. When he got back with the milk he dipped the can right into the lake to wash the mud off the jacket. In those days the milk was shipped from Remsen. In order to keep the milk cool the cans were covered with a two-inch-thick jacket of insulation, fastened with straps and buckles. And so even with a mud bath the milk was in good condition.

There is another favorite story in the family, about the guests who could neither walk the distance from Big Moose to Twitchell nor ride over the rough road in the buckboard:

They [the guests] had to be carried in by means of an armchair with two poles under the seat attached by rope to the boat yokes, which the men use on their shoulders when carrying a heavy load. It took two men — one in the front, one at the back — to carry the chair.

One guest had a very narrow escape while being carried in this way from the lake to the Station. Without giving any advance notice that she would like a few of the wildflowers along the side of the trail, she reached over to pick them. This so threw the men off balance that they had a wild scramble to keep her from falling out of the chair. They managed to hold the chair upright until they could set it on firm ground. When they stopped to rest the man in front turned around and said to this passenger, "Lady, don't do that again, as the next time you might not be as lucky, for some of those holes are real deep, and you might need a bath!"

Someone else gives his impression of the early years at Twitchell: "The first I recall of Earl was when my wife, my son and I began going to Twitchell Lake Inn, traveling over a woods-road by buckboard, which met all the passenger trains at Big Moose Station. ... The reception by Earl Covey and his wife when we arrived at the

The Twitchell Years

The railroad fueled the increasing appeal of the Adirondacks as a place for vacations and development. The New York Central's Adirondack Division was built in the 1890's with the Big Moose Station one of the earliest stops on the line. The railroad passed within sight of Big Moose Lake. The station was about two miles away, and the Big Moose Transportation Company operated teams of horses to carry passengers to and from the lake. By the 1920's, the peak of the rail service to the area, there were ten passenger trains a day and regular freight service through Big Moose Station. A small village emerged, and a bus had replaced the horses.

hotel was so genuine that it endeared Twitchell Lake Inn to me and my family forever."

Whenever Earl met a new guest at the Station he delighted in being immediately able to address the stranger by name, having nothing to guide him other than correspondence relative to accommodations at the Inn. This correspondence usually gave Earl some idea of the kind of person he was to meet. To the guest, it must have been as heart-warming as it was surprising to be met thus by his cheery, friendly host.

Earl's guests were impressed in the beginning not so much by his appearance as by his energy and his willingness to tackle any kind of job, no matter how difficult. What he lacked in physical stature, being of less than average height, he more than made up in his capacity for work. When he did pause for a visit now and then, one noted the high forehead, the deep-set blue eyes, the firm mouth and chin, the clear-cut profile. It was a face honest and kind, the face of a man who could be trusted.

Early Building

Despite the fact that the old road was little better than a trail, guests were coming to the Inn in increasing numbers, making it necessary to enlarge the dining room and add sleeping rooms upstairs. Cottages were built one by one, and a boathouse, a barn and a shop were added as time and money permitted. The main house and the first cottages were built of half logs, with spruce battens covering the joints. Later Earl used bark-covered slabs nailed to sheathing with a layer of waterproof paper between; the inside was finished with paneling of spruce or birch. Until he had his own sawmill in 1910, his lumber, mostly rough material, was sawed at Dart's.

When Earl could not afford a helper he worked alone, sometimes working at night if Addie needed his help in the kitchen during the day. Once, pressed for time when building a boathouse up the lake, he worked for thirteen days and nights almost without stopping. He did the same on one of the cottages at the Inn. He did much of his night work at the barn, which was new then and far enough away to keep the sounds of hammer and saw from disturbing his guests.

Frequently a late spring or early winter kept him working against time and the weather. Putting a roof on a new building before the coming of winter made it possible to continue the inside finishing without interruption thus making a difference of months in the time required to complete the job.

On two occasions Earl built cottages on very short notice. When one of his guests very much wanted a cottage at a time when they were all occupied, "Earl immediately went to work," we are told, "and put up part of a cottage ... in a few days' time so that she [the guest} was able to have a cottage most of that vacation." For another guest, who arrived unexpectedly at a time when the Inn was full, Earl built a cottage in a day. Earl was always generous with his time, and when one of his friends wanted a home at the Station, Earl drew the plans and helped with the building, making no charge for his part of the work.

A former camper writes: "One spring we found he had built a little camp near the kitchen for a schoolhouse, and there was a schoolteacher living at the Inn teaching the five Covey children and two Brownells, the minimum number for whom the State would provide a teacher."

She continues: "When he was planning to build a big camp for my mother [Mrs. Hayes] I remember well how he found the best spring, walking across the back of the lots with a witch-hopple [or dowsing] fork, which turned down where there was water. When he was building the fireplaces he took the train to White Lake, picked the stone, huge boulders, loaded them onto freight cars, came back, unloaded them when they arrived and took them to camp. Then we would hear the sound of his chipping the stone all day long as he worked — nothing seemed too hard or difficult for him."

Another friend and Twitchell neighbor relates his experience in acquiring property at the lake. Three lots adjacent to the Inn were owned by two men, one living in Old Forge, the other at Raquette Lake. The Kitendaughs, after spending their vacations at the Inn for several years, became interested in these lots. The Old Forge owner was willing to sell, but at first the Raquette Lake man was not. Finally, however, the latter also agreed to sell, and one day Earl appeared at the Mansion House in Kenwoode [3.] to let the Kitendaughs know that the lots were available.

To continue in Mr. Kitendaugh's own words:

> Several hours were then spent by Earl in making sketches of the proposed camp with outdoor sleeping porch, water line from his reservoir and especially the fireplace.
> In those days the trains ran from Old Forge to Raquette Lake but three times a week. After leaving my home with the camp plans, Earl had gone home and later taken a train to Raquette Lake, secured signature to deed, etc., then although it was midwinter and a blizzard he would not waste a day or two waiting for a train, but walked home ... probably on the railroad track itself or the old road from Raquette Lake to Eagle Bay.

[3.] Near Oneida, New York.

Earl Covey was as at home on the water as he was in the woods. Photo dated 1903.

In any case he reached the upper end of Big Moose Lake, and it must have been after dark for he arrived home at 2 a.m. In crossing Big Moose Lake in the blizzard, he got the full force of the wind, which up to then had been moderated by the trees, so he had to take off his coat to wind around his nose and ears to keep them from freezing. He succeeded in both crossing the lake and covering the two and a half miles farther to Twitchell Lake. I don't know yet how he did it. However, he had cut the timber off much of this land in earlier days and was noted for having built a skidway over one valley, top of the mountain and the next valley to get his logs to Big Moose Lake, which is something I never heard of another woodsman doing.

When my family arrived with me on Decoration Day, the camp was built and far better than promised. ... The fireplace with its marvelous stone mantel, with keystone and wonderfully matching colored stone on either side, made it complete.

Another camper pays her grateful tribute: "Earl did so much for us. Especially our lovely fireplace. All he was told was: 'Have it big enough and lovely to look at, for we will use it so much.' And look what he created."

This fireplace was among the first that Earl built and was one of his finest. At the same camp he also built a large lean-to. "So lots of people can get together and sing" were the only instructions given him. "He was never told what size to make it. That was left to him. At times as many as thirty-two people, mostly children, gathered in that lean-to and sang before the open campfire."

An old-time guest and friend gave her impressions of the early years at the Inn: "The first time I saw Earl was in the spring of 1908, when I first visited Twitchell with my father and mother. He had five small children then, and the Inn was much smaller, and there were only two cottages, the big one next to the Inn and the one on the Point as I remember. Also there was a small boathouse."

In about 1906 the children of Earl and Addie Covey were (L-R) William Earl (born December 1895), Emma (born January 1897), Mildred (born August 1899), Sumner Burt (born October 1901) and Henry (born July 1903). Photo taken at Twitchell

As the family returned from year to year: "We saw progress from kerosene angle lamps to acetylene, to electricity. Every innovation meant Earl had to know all about the installation and maintenance needed. And the plumbing for the place! He started from scratch and put up the buildings. I was always impressed by his versatility."

When people asked again and again, "How did you learn to do all of this?" Earl would answer, "I had to."

When there was work to be done and no one else to do it or even to show him how, from sheer necessity he had to learn by doing it

Earl Covey after a successful hunting trip in 1909 or 1910.

himself. Thus he early acquired a degree of knowledge and skill, which was a continual source of wonder and admiration to his friends and associates.

Someone said:

> I have never known a man with more accomplishments than Earl Covey. He seemed to know how to do almost anything and to do it perfectly.
> I shall never forget how expert he was with an ax. I think he could almost split a hair. I remember there were some people from New York who had their golf clubs with them. They were hitting some old balls out into the lake down at the boathouse and persuaded Earl to try and hit one of them. And so with his expert ax swing he knocked it clear across the lake, which is very unusual for anybody who never had a golf club in his hands before. And what a woodsman he was. He had the instinct of an Indian in the woods. He seemed to be absolutely tireless.

Host and Guide

Each year as the Lake became better known, the number of campers increased, and in addition to his responsibilities at the Inn Earl was building private camps. He cut wood for the campers and filled their ice houses. His four-seated "top-wagon" [4] met them at the Station when they arrived and took them to the train when they departed. They bought groceries at the Inn and there sent out and received their mail. During the early years, when there were few if any others around to perform the services required by campers, Earl literally had to be "all things to all men."

Here are some comments from people who knew Earl:

"Whenever one of the woodsmen had an accident he always went to Earl who knew what to do."

"He was never too busy to answer a child's questions or to help someone needing assistance."

"Earl would lend us anything he had — always ready to help and

---

[4] So-called from the canopy over the seats; also known as "mountain wagon."

always with a smile. He was quiet in voice and manner, never shouted at anyone. Everyone was devoted to him."

Addie's close friend and neighbor pays this tribute:

> The outstanding traits of his [Earl's] life were his kindness and thoughtfulness of others, the day-by-day living a life of usefulness. Always ready to help in times of trouble or emergency. He was quick to think and act on anything that would give pleasure or comfort to others.
>
> One time on the spur of the moment, learning that I had never been to Blue Mountain Lake, he sent Addie and me on an excursion to the lake. He sent the team to meet us on our return,[5] and halfway back we found him by the side of the road with a wonderful steak dinner for us — the kind of thing one never forgets.

Mr. Eugene Kitendaugh tells his story of meals cooked and served: "In early days no meat was carried into Twin Sisters [6] and each hunter came out with his buck. It seemed to me that the last dinner was the best of all. Earl would take all the odds and ends of food in the camp, put them together in a kettle, boil them for an hour or two and turn out by some magic a hunter's stew that had no equal in the food line in the Parker House or Waldorf Astoria."

Mr. Kitendaugh goes on to tell of another meal that Earl prepared for him and a friend who in the past had entertained him at the Adirondack League Club. It was in the fall, when the autumn colors were at the height of their beauty.

> We planned to take my friend to the Inlet of Big Moose Lake where there was a gorgeous view of lake, mountain and stream, with all the colors of fall, and there Earl was to cook one of his wonderful meals. But on the morning of the day we were to leave, my friend woke up with a cold and sore throat and so did not want to go outdoors.
>
> That did not stop Earl and a wonderful dinner. He did not deign
> to use the kitchen range and other conveniences of the kitchen but

---

[5] Probably the women were met at Eagle Bay.
[6] Twin Sister Lakes, more than five miles from Twitchell.

built a large hardwood fire in my marvelous fireplace that he had built in earlier days and then on the wood coals cooked before our eyes a finer dinner than my friend had ever eaten in any of the many camps of the Adirondack League Club.

Mr. Kitendaugh's guest apparently enjoyed the meal despite his cold. The unique circumstances of its cooking may have lent an added flavor. But the food was good to begin with. Earl would never have anything but the best. He knew moreover, how to cook it. Steak or chicken broiled under his watchful eye made a meal of something one never forgot.

As years passed the Covey hospitality and good food became well known. In those days there was telephone connection of a sort between the Inn and Big Moose Lake. Sometimes there would be a call from Big Moose Lake ordering a steak dinner for from ten to twenty people. It was almost always possible to have the meal on the date desired. On arrival of the dinner guests Earl and Addie would be outside the door waiting to greet them.

One young couple after their wedding at Big Moose Lake was to leave for their honeymoon by train the next morning. They spent their first night at Twitchell. A cottage was ready for them on their arrival at the Inn. Even the curtains were drawn. Was there anything else they wanted? Earl asked.

Assured that they would be very comfortable, Earl bade them good night. The next morning he drove them to the train, which took them on their way. The friend who told this story made the comment that "there was nothing about Earl that was not good."

Working night after night to complete a cottage, carrying supplies to a hunting party camping at the Sisters, going at night by trail through the woods, Earl seemed, as someone remarked, "absolutely tireless."

Earl was "always ready to help in times of trouble or emergency." A guest had a ring, which was too tight; it was filed off. A man injured in the woods received first aid. A smile, cheery word, lending a hand. All were part of his day's work.

Earl's services as a guide on hunting trips were highly valued. A woman on one of the trips he guided said of him: "He was a wonderful hunter. He never spared himself and always made us so comfortable."

Mrs. Beatrice Herben gives us her early recollections of Earl:

> The first impressive memory was established by my father, Dr. Louis E. Slayton, who responded to someone's assertion that "Earl Covey is a very shy man" with an emphatic "No, he is not shy. He is modest."
>
> Through the years of our associations with him as a most friendly and helpful neighbor, as the maker of the Slayton fireplace, the builder of the first Herben Camp and the second Herben Camp, which is our own home, his essential quality remained modesty, which was the more endearing in that it in no way diminished his authority in his own fields.
>
> The second memory also dates from the earliest years: In 1904 my mother first came to Twitchell. She walked the hard way carrying in her long skirt a ten-month-old baby, over a muddy and stony road — the old road, which went over and not around the mountain lying between Big Moose Station and Twitchell Lake.
>
> It was dark, raining and cold.
>
> "At the Inn dock," said my mother, "Mr. Covey assured us that he would bring our trunks up in the morning. The Lake looked very black … He helped me into the rowboat, long dress, ruined shoes, baby and all. … I shall not forget the courage he gave to us as he said quietly, 'Do not be afraid. You'll find your way all right and there'll be a light in the first cove, beyond the island. There'll be a light!' And there was a light and a fire burning for us!"

Sometimes there were calls for help, which stretched the days into the hours of the night. One afternoon two Twitchell neighbors went hunting. Before they realized the lateness of the hour, darkness had overtaken them, and having neither lantern nor flashlight they could not find their way back.

When the men failed to return by suppertime Mrs. Kitendaugh went to the Inn to report their absence. Earl immediately went out and fired shots from a rifle hoping the hunters would hear and fire answering shots in return so that he could locate them. But a high hill between intercepted the sound, and Earl's shots were not heard. Meanwhile there were other shots from the direction of North Bay, which the Kitendaughs did hear and which they answered. It was not long before they were joined by a third hunter, also lost. His were the shots that came from North Bay.

Receiving no response to his rifle shots, Earl set out in search of the Kitendaughs. He got into a boat and rowed up the lake to a spot near Noble's camp. Here he went ashore and, leaving the boat, started over the trail through the woods. He finally came upon the three men at the end of South Pond swamp, standing before an open fire.

When the hunter from North Bay saw that Earl and the Kitendaughs were starting toward Twitchell he was much displeased. He wanted to go to North Bay, even when he was told that the walk to Twitchell would be easier and that Earl would take him from there to Big Moose Lake without charging for the trip. Still somewhat disgruntled, the stranger decided to accompany the others. From the Inn Earl, as agreed, drove him the rest of his way home.

There was the time when three rifle shots were heard in the night from the upper end of Twitchell. Again making a trip up the lake by boat, Earl found that Low Hamilton was ill and needed a physician. Earl rowed back to the Inn, hitched up the team and drove to the Station to call a doctor in Old Forge. Then instead of returning to the Inn he waited at the Station for the remainder of the night, met the doctor arriving on the early morning train and took him to Twitchell. Low Hamilton afterward remarked: "I knew that if Earl Covey heard the shots, he'd come."

The Twitchell years, years of ceaseless toil though they were, had their lighter moments. Earl loved fishing and hunting. While he enjoyed spending much of his time at these sports as a guide, he nevertheless enjoyed almost as much seeing others get pleasure from them. As a matter of fact, even in his free time Earl seldom went alone. He always knew of someone who would be delighted to accompany him, and bringing pleasure to someone else added to his own enjoyment.

Near the end of the season, when there were no parties to guide, Earl's hunting trips with a few friends were real events. There had to be a camp, far back in the woods, which would provide adequate shelter for four or five men for the better part of a week. Supplies of food, bedding and even a stove had to be carried in. This entailed one trip before hand and sometimes more. [7.] The story is told that Earl himself carried a stove to the hunting camp. After he had covered a considerable distance over a trail one of the other men offered to relieve him of his load. Earl refused the offer, saying that his shoulders were already so numb that it didn't matter, he didn't feel it anyway, and on he went, still carrying the stove.

They were hard work, those hunting trips, but what good times the men had. His friends still remember the cupboard he built out of two broken guide boats, the meals he cooked, the stories he told. One of Earl's companions tells of trips made when the men left from Big Moose Lake:

> Mr. Covey was a wonderful man to go hunting with. What he didn't know about hunting no one else knew. I have had some wonderful trips with him.
>
> I will never forget one of them. We left Big Moose Lake one Saturday afternoon at 4 p.m. and arrived at camp on Upper Sister Lake at 6:30 p.m., which at that time of year is 'way after dark. We traveled by lantern light; we made as good time in the dark as we did in daylight. The next morning we were up early; Mr. Covey always got breakfast and what a breakfast. Ham and eggs and flapjacks. He could make the best flapjacks I've ever eaten. On another trip we left Big Moose Lake late in the afternoon for the Upper Sister. There were four of us. We had no camp to stay in, but that did not bother Mr. Covey any. He said we would build something after we got there.
>
> We arrived just at dark, and by 8 p.m. we had a lean-to erected, which I thought was quite a feat. It was quite chilly around the corners at night, but we made out very nicely and continued our week's hunting from there.
>
> After a day's hunt, while Mr. Covey got supper, the rest of us cut wood to keep warm at night. That required a lot of wood for a lean-to. After supper was over we would listen to Mr. Covey and his yarns about the experiences he had had hunting bear and deer, and there were many.
>
> On one of our hunting trips we had lots of snow and 18

[7.] Canned goods not opened during the hunting trip were buried and then used the following year.

degrees below zero before the week was over. Both the Sister Lakes were frozen as was the marsh (part of the inlet to Big Moose Lake), strong enough to walk on. Our deer were frozen so hard we couldn't bend them to make a pack to carry, so we dragged them all the way down on the ice to Big Moose Lake, which was still open. That was a pretty rugged hunting trip, but Mr. Covey did not seem to mind it at all.

At the Inn in the early days there were exciting canoe races, log-rolling contests, taffy pulls and popcorn parties. Someone recalls: "When taffy was made, it was Earl who knew when to take the syrup off the stove and when the taffy was ready."

Probably for the guests, certainly for Earl, the red-letter events of the summer were the square dances, held in the dining room of the Inn before the living room was enlarged to its present size. There was nothing he more thoroughly enjoyed or entered into more wholeheartedly than square dancing. The rhythm, the variety of movement, the sharing of his enjoyment with others, seeing so many having such a good time, made of it a favorite form of recreation with him as long as he lived.

No one was too old or too young to attend Earl's square dances. Everyone was welcome. There were guests, campers and square-dance enthusiasts from neighboring communities. Even the babies were brought by their parents and put to sleep lying cross-wise on the beds upstairs. The older children, four and five years old, watched the dancing as long as they could keep awake. Then, crawling under the chairs, they too went to sleep.

As described by one friend, there were "guides in their woods clothes and campers in knickers and a man with an accordion to furnish the music." When it came time to start dancing the call went out: "Get your partners for the quadrille!" And the dancers in "square sets," four couples to a set, began to fill the floor. For the final set: "Four more couples!" A last call: "One more couple!" Then, with everyone in place, Earl gave the signal for the music to begin, and the dance was on.

A long-time friend and Twitchell camper recalls her memories of the dances and the dancers:

One small boy was dressed up for the occasion in high-laced shoes, black cotton stockings, dark blue breeches, a white blouse with a square collar and wearing an enormous red bow-tie.

The dances were done briskly but in perfect rhythm, the ladies swaying back and forth to show their ruffled petticoats. One of them wore beautiful high button shoes of patent leather with cloth tops. The music allowed plenty of time for the men to put in clog steps that grew louder and louder as the evening wore on. Although everyone had worked hard all day, no one was too tired for a square dance. The upright piano was pulled out from the wall so that Fred Pierce, who not only called but also played the fiddle, kept a spittoon behind the piano for his use. After dancing we went out onto the porch through the windows, wide open at the bottom.

When it came time for the midnight supper, the children were chased back inside, and the tables, long boards on supports, were set the length and width of the room. The meal consisted of baked beans, potato salad, cold ham, pickles, jelly, hot rolls, coleslaw, bowls of hard-boiled eggs, tea, coffee, old-fashioned home-made custard ice cream made in a hand freezer and many high frosted cakes.

After supper Earl would say, "You can't go home yet," and the music would start again, and the dancing resume. This went on until four or five o'clock in the morning.

When the new barn was finished, Earl invited everyone to a square dance on its clean floor. Ice cream and cake were brought from the house. The babies were put to sleep in the new hay overhead. That is the way the barn was christened. All of this required much work on the part of the Coveys. But to Earl nothing was too much trouble if people had a good time.

Once during the winter Earl came home after working all day and helped to shovel snow to clear a place near the house before a square dance. After the party there was so little time left for sleep that he simply changed his clothes, hitched up the team and started off the next morning for another day's work. On another occasion everybody went to a party, danced all night, worked the next day and went to another party the second night. By the third night the dancers were ready to go to bed early.

A friend of Earl's, himself a square-dance enthusiast, recalls the parties he attended:

The music of those dances, if it could only be reproduced. And Mr. Covey calling and dancing, and Mr. Covey dancing the schottische. Those were real community parties, with square dancing as an American folk dance at its best. What pleasure they gave to the participants. What memories those have who were present at all of them through the years.

Mr. Covey was one of those comparatively few, I think, who are really inspired by square dancing. He loved it. He responded so completely to the message it has to give, and he could hand that message on to others.

For Earl, square dancing was more than a mere pastime. Strenuous though it was, the rhythmic movement to a lively tune brought relaxation and relief from the daily routine. On one occasion, not at a square dance, while carrying one of his grandchildren, he half-walked, half-waltzed about the room, humming to himself a familiar dance tune. The very sound of it set his feet to dancing, even with a baby in his arms.

A boyhood friend of Earl's son, William, summed up the Twitchell years as he knew them from his personal contact with Earl:

> I must have been all of fourteen years old when I first met Earl Covey. To me he was almost a god.
> In my young mind, there was nothing Mr. Covey could not do. The better I got to know him, the more that became apparent. He was a distinguished carpenter, an expert pipefitter, a stonemason, a road builder, a buckboard driver and an automobile mechanic.
> These things he had to do to keep the Twitchell Lake Inn running. I well remember my parents' genuine concern lest Mr. Covey work himself to death. His saw and hammer were often going before daylight, and he never came in to the office to sit down till long after dark.
> Despite his constant duties at the Inn, he found time to fish and hunt and the many deer heads on the walls of the Inn proved that he was a dead shot with a rifle.
> I was fortunate enough to accompany him to the hunting camp he was building not far from the shores of Shingle Shanty Pond. There he worked fast and skillfully with a minimum of tools. He

erected a snug, level camp in short order, in which I later spent a week in midwinter with his son, Willie, who operated a trapping line from it. We were warm and dry there despite sub-zero weather.

As I grew older, the "Mr." finally changed to Earl, but it was the man I knew when I was a boy who is today clearest in my mind. One of the treats he provided was the bass-fishing trip he took Francis Noble and me on to Eighth Lake.

We drove over through Eagle Bay in a car and by guide-boat up the Fulton Chain. He threw up a lean-to in no time when we got to Eighth and provided lively crawfish for bait. He'd gathered them from under rocks on the point off the boathouse.

The bass came fast and furious, and Francis and I had the time of our lives. I think Earl had a good time just watching us. At least, he hogged none of the sport.

I have seen Earl at work with tough woodsmen and at the oars of a guideboat filled with ladies. He was the same in both places. I never heard him swear or tell an off-color story. I think he had a sense of innate pride, but I never saw him show off, and I never heard him brag.

He had a personality, which refused to be beaten down by hard work. He always danced with glee and grace at the Inn square dances and was as light as a feather on his feet. He was adept at the waltz, running with a funny little skip when it came time to reverse, and in a schottische his feet positively flashed. His generosity was fabulous. He automatically extended a helping hand to anyone who was down on his luck. No one stayed hungry very long in his presence. Older folk used to say he gave away all his profits.

Not all of them. For the bulk of his profits was not in dollars and cents. He had memories that were his own. There are still people who cannot see the glowing coals of an open hardwood fire without thinking of Earl Covey.

And so the Twitchell years passed. They were years of hard work, with now and then brief times for play. There were five children in the family. When they were old enough to play by themselves, they would take their lunch and, with younger children in the care of the older ones, all would go to some outdoor spot to spend the day while their parents were busy at the Inn. As the children grew older they learned to help with the work, giving Earl more time for building. The details of the resort business were left more and more in the capable hands of Addie Covey, assisted by the young people in the family. Earl did not like chores nor did he have any inclination for deskwork, but in an emergency or time of special need he was ready to step in and help.

Until 1910, when he built his own sawmill, Earl hauled logs to other mills to be sawed into lumber. The only serious loss he incurred at Twitchell was four years later, 1914, when the sawmill was destroyed by fire. It had been a very dry season. One man usually remained at the mill during the noon hour while the others were at dinner. One day when no one was there a fire broke out and not even the desperate efforts of everyone on the place, including the woman's bucket brigade from the lake to the burning building, could save it. The mill and the lumber already sawed were a total loss. Earl had to purchase material, which he needed immediately, to replace that which was burned. Fortunately, no one suffered injury, and later Earl rebuilt the sawmill.

Building work continued to occupy much of his time. His services as a builder were in constant and growing demand at Twitchell, at Big Moose Lake and even in Canada. He was becoming well known for his fireplaces, which not only contributed to one's physical comfort but added beauty to otherwise plain and simple rooms. From the skill of the artisan — never was there a Covey fireplace, which did not "draw" well, never in his stonework did he leave a tool-mark showing — was emerging the artist's sense of color, line and proportion. Greater possibilities in the use of his native wood and stone were opening up before Earl.

Building in Canada

It is not surprising therefore that building was becoming a dominant interest in his life, even to the point of taking him at times away from Twitchell. In 1916 he contracted for two jobs, one for Henry Milligan of Big Moose Lake and the other for Edward Brandagee on a lake about a hundred miles north of the city of Quebec, Canada. Dovetailing the one with the other, Earl completed both jobs by the summer of 1917.

Earl Covey's skills as a builder led him to a project building a camp for Edward Brandagee on a lake about a hundred miles north of Quebec City. On June 5, 1917, Earl set out in a Model T Ford with his daughter Emma to do the cooking and John Buckley who could speak French. Some of the roads presented extraordinary difficulty.

The building of the camp in Canada is a story in itself. Before Earl could begin building the Brandagee camp, much had to be done by way of preparation. In the fall of 1916 he shipped lumber, doors and windows to Baie St. Paul for the job. From there, when there was enough snow to make the drawing easy, he took the material to the campsite. On the same trip he took canned goods that would keep through the winter, burying them in a pit, which he covered well to prevent freezing. It was then too early to get ice from the lake, so he put snow into an ice house he built for the purpose. By the following summer the snow had formed a chunk of ice large enough to provide refrigeration from early June till late August.

On the morning of June 5, 1917, Earl left Twitchell in a Model T Ford, taking with him his daughter Emma to do the cooking and John Buckley, who could speak French. Because they were to be miles from the nearest town, they had to take with them everything they might need. A snapshot of the three in the car, on returning

Having sent lumber, doors and windows in the fall of 1916, Covey was able to complete the Brandagee house as planned, and the travelers returned to Twitchell Lake none the worse for the experience. They arrived back on August 21st with hunting trophies and a well worn coffee pot hanging from the side of the automobile.

from Canada, shows the Model T loaded with their goods and chattels and bearing a large coffee pot in a conspicuous place on one side because there was nowhere else to put it.

It was a four-day trip from Twitchell to the site of the camp. From Quebec to Port Lewis, which took four days, they kept to the south side of the river to avoid driving through snow still covering the ground on the opposite side. At Port Lewis they ferried across to Baie St. Paul and thence to St. Urbain.

At the time when Earl took the Ford to Canada the automobile was comparatively unknown. As he drove through the countryside on the way to St. Urbain, chickens near by, startled at the sound of the car, scattered in every direction. Children playing beside the road were frightened at the strange object coming toward them and ran to the house as fast as they could go. Never before had they seen anything like this queer carriage, moving along faster than any horse could run. The Ford was going twenty-five miles an hour.

At St. Urbain, Earl arranged to have supplies carried to the camp by horse and buckboard. He planned to drive the Ford for another ten miles, going the remainder of the way in the buckboard. With this plan in mind the party started out from St. Urbain. The car went first, with the horse-drawn buckboard following.

A mile and a half or two miles out of the village they came to a hill. The Ford started the ascent, but the sticky clay proved to be too much for the Model T. Unable to get the car up the hill, the party could do nothing but turn around and go back to St. Urbain. At this point the horse, seeing the car coming toward it, became so frightened that it had to be unhitched and taken back into the woods until the car had gone on out of sight. When the horse was finally brought back and rehitched to the buckboard, that, too, was taken back to St. Urbain.

Leaving the Ford, the three passengers started out from St. Urbain once more, this time in the buckboard. After a rather uncomfortable trip, they reached the camp, which was some twenty miles away. Anyone who has ever ridden in a buckboard (with no springs) can testify that to ride that far over a road such as can only be traveled in a buckboard, is an endurance test of the first order.

The travelers, however, arrived at their destination apparently none the worse for their experience. Work on the building began and proceeded without interruption. By August 21st, the camp finished, Earl and his fellow workers returned to Twitchell.

William Covey

It was in April of that year that the United States entered World War I. Earl's eldest son, William, now past the age of twenty-one, was eligible for the draft. On June 5, the day that his father left for Canada, Bill registered for military service.

During Bill's course of training at Camp Devens, Massachusetts, members of the family visited him. On one of their trips they brought him some jerked venison. To have literally a "taste of the woods" before leaving for overseas must have meant more to him than he had words to express. Bill liked venison, he liked hunting, and he was a good woodsman. With experience as a guide, and with his sense of direction, he could reach a spot to which there was no trail by going straight through the woods. Like many woodsmen he was somewhat reserved, not given to much talk. But he declared that that jerked venison was the best he ever tasted. Not long afterward he was sent over with a division that transported supplies by truck to the front lines.

In the government's drive for the sale of Liberty Bonds following this country's entry into the war, the community of Big Moose did its full share. Two Big Moose boys, Bill Covey and Thomas Marleau, had been inducted into the armed forces, which gave Earl as chairman of the drive for that area added incentive to sell as many bonds as possible. He sold many more than the quota assigned to him, mostly to local residents.

The year of 1918 was the year when the deadly Spanish influenza swept two continents, taking a heavy toll of lives. Bill, serving with the armed forces in Europe, was one of its victims. News of his death on December 3, 1918, after a brief illness in a French hospital, was received at Twitchell a few days later. The place of his burial was one of the national cemeteries in France, which had been set aside for Americans who lost their lives in the armed conflict. Bill was gone from home for more than a year. Occasionally there had come a letter from him, which, though it could give little actual information, at least let the family know that he was still alive. And there had always been the hope that he would return. There would be no more letters, and Bill was not coming back.

In their nearly twenty years at Twitchell the Coveys had met with very little misfortune. The burning of the sawmill was perhaps their most serious loss. Now that they were seeing the results of their years of hard work in the steady growth of the Inn, they had been able to look forward to the future with reasonable confidence. The World War and Bill's absence overseas had been the only dark shadows on their horizon.

Suddenly they were forced to adjust to the fact that they would not see Bill again. There would be an emptiness in their lives, which no one else could fill. Gradually, as they went about their daily tasks — then, if never before, they must have been thankful for work, which kept them busy — the aching sorrow was eased, and they learned to accept the loss of their son.

Addie Covey, as did many other parents whose sons were buried in France, wanted the body of her son brought home. To this end she began corresponding with government authorities in Washington, receiving blanks and questionnaires to be filled out and returned. After a period of more than two years, Bill's body was finally brought back.

At the end of the war a chapter of the American Legion in Old Forge was named the William Covey Post in Bill's memory. (Years later it was renamed the Covey-Pashley Post, to honor also William Pashley of Old Forge, who died in World War II.)

After Bill's death someone conceived the idea of a memorial to him at Twitchell Lake. One of his favorite spots as a boy had been Twitchell Lake outlet, where the bridge crossed the stream. He and other boys had spent many hours at play there. Twitchell friends suggested that in place of the wooden structure then spanning the outlet, a bridge built of stone be erected as a memorial to Bill. In 1921 the present bridge over Twitchell Outlet was completed and dedicated to the memory of William Covey. To pay for the building of the bridge two of Bill's friends, Francis Noble and George Murray, set about raising the necessary funds. For a year or more they received contributions from friends and guests of the Coveys.

Addition to the Inn

Meanwhile, deciding that the growth of the business called for more adequate accommodations at the Inn, Earl proceeded with work on an addition to the main house. By removing the partition between the old sitting room and the men's smoking room, and by extending the easterly end of the building beyond the porch on that side, he made one large living room. He used yellow birch to panel its walls. The floor was so laid that in the nearly forty years that followed it remained tight without buckling and was a source of lasting pride to its builder.

But the addition did not stop there. New guest rooms with private baths appeared on the second floor. The rebuilding of the verandah included four private balcony-porches for the rooms overhead. The wooden steps in the front were replaced by stone.

Finally, though there still seemed to be no end to the hard work, life for the Coveys had become somewhat easier. They had come through their pioneering years, when with little more than their willing hands and stout hearts they had overcome one obstacle after another. Improved methods of lightening the burden of toil were coming into use at Twitchell. While the growth of the Inn necessitated outside help — a cook, a laundress and waitresses and chambermaids — the business was still a family affair in which the younger Coveys worked with the others. Earl devoted most of his time to building, either at the Inn or on other jobs. Having no interest in routine business detail, he left all of that for Addie. She assumed it along with her housekeeping responsibilities.

Cheerful, brisk and a hard worker who was first in one place and then another, Addie was to be found wherever her assistance and supervision were most needed. Sometimes she filled in herself if there was a shortage of help — something that was more than likely to occur at the height of the season. Such was the case in the summer of 1920, when for some reason the Coveys were without a cook. Addie stepped in to fill the place temporarily in the hope that Earl would succeed in finding someone else for the job. But no one could be found, and Addie continued to do the cooking for the remainder of the summer.

Always strong and well, Addie Covey had never known sickness until the early fall of that year, when she suddenly became ill. Finally she entered the hospital in Albany, New York, where the trouble was diagnosed as a fibroid tumor. Surgery was required.

Unfortunately, after the operation pneumonia developed. Addie did not recover. After a week's illness she died, on September 22, 1920.

When Addie Covey had gone to Twitchell Lake twenty-one years before, she cooked, cleaned, washed, ironed and brought up her family with little outside help and none of the conveniences of modern living. At first she cleaned and filled kerosene lamps. Then came acetylene gas for lights and finally electricity. She lived through the bowl-and-pitcher era to see private baths installed with guest-

Earl and Addie's son William died of the Spanish influenza while serving in France during World War I. Earl designed and constructed this bridge as a memorial to his lost son. Not far from the Twitchell Lake Inn the setting where the old bridge crossed the outlet had always been one of William's favorite places. The bridge was dedicated in 1921.

rooms. She saw the Inn, grow from one building to a resort with cottages, a boathouse and accommodations for fifty or more people. By the end of Addie's life a new road had been built to the Lake from the Station. Here and there the automobile was beginning to replace the horse-drawn carriage. Through it all Twitchell Lake Inn retained its charm. There was still the simple comfort, the friendly atmosphere. It was still the quiet, lovely place it had always been, in large measure because of Addie Covey's work and watchful care.

With Addie gone, Earl had little further interest in the Inn. Mildred and Sumner, the two eldest of the children then at home, assumed responsibility for managing it in their mother's place. During the winter that followed Earl got out pulpwood for Charles Williams, a hotel man at Big Moose Lake. A sawmill was set up for the purpose at the Station, and Earl spent most of the winter there with his friends the Denios.

The Memorial Bridge

By the spring of 1921 there was enough money from contributions to enable Earl to begin work on the memorial bridge at the Outlet. The funds were to pay for material and the men's wages. Earl gave his time. Stone came from the White Lake quarry by train to Big Moose and was drawn from there by team to Twitchell. Skilled stoneworkers were brought from a quarry in Barre, Vermont, to help cut and lay the stone.

Toward the end of the summer the bridge was complete, and a date was set for its dedication. The return of William Covey's body from France only a few weeks before added poignantly to the occasion. On August 27, 1921, members of the family, friends and guests at the Inn, campers from every part of the lake and members of the local American Legion met at the bridge to honor the memory of the young man who had gone from Twitchell to answer his country's call.

The simple ceremony was planned and conducted by close friends. They paid tribute to the soldier they had known from boyhood. There was the raising of the flag, an address in dedication of the bridge and in closing the singing of "America" followed by the Benediction. Some of those present lingered afterward to read the inscriptions on two bronze tablets, placed one on each side of the bridge.

On driving up the last hill toward Twitchell one makes a final turn in the road. There, spanning the Twitchell Lake Outlet, is the bridge. With its low protecting wall in long pieces of cut stone, undergirded by a supporting arch over the stream, it stands in simplicity, strength and lasting beauty as if it has been there always.

The Death of Henry

During the summer of 1921 Earl's sons, Sumner and Henry, helped their father in the building of the bridge. Henry, however, did not feel well. He spent most of his time at the bridge, watching others work when unable to do much himself. As the weeks passed he suffered increasingly from what felt like a "stiff neck." Finally in

September Earl took Henry to the Faxton Hospital in Utica in the hope of finding the cause of the trouble. Doctors there, unable to discover what was wrong, could not help. After a week in which his condition grew steadily worse, Henry died on October 5, 1921. He was eighteen.

An autopsy revealed that a vertebra in the boy's neck was perforated. How long this condition had existed, or what caused it, was a mystery. When he was about thirteen years old Henry was in a car that overturned going downhill. He felt no ill effects at the time and seemed in perfect health until his last illness. So far as the family could recall, this was the only incident that might have caused the condition that ultimately led to his death.

In the space of three short years, death claimed three of Earl's family. Now again, as twice before, he carried the burden of sorrow as he returned to work. But, so quietly and patiently did he bear it that, were it not for the quick tears that appeared at the mention of a loved one who had been taken, one would scarcely suspect the impact his loss had made upon him.

Naturally reticent in matters that deeply affected him, Earl was equally so in his expression of sympathy to others. If told of someone else's loss he would reply simply, "Is that so?" But those brief words were so gently, so kindly spoken that one immediately sensed his sympathy and understanding. It was all Earl needed to say.

The times of sorrow interrupted Earl's work only for brief periods. He continued to be as busy as he had always been. Life went on, but no longer was it the same. He felt alone and lost. He thought that after building two more cottages at the Inn, he might go to California.

Chapter III

A Fresh Start

The reason for the apparent digression at this point is that the writer now becomes part of the Earl Covey story. This is how it happened:

Summer of 1922

That was the summer when I saw Twitchell Lake for the first time. I had spent two years in Syracuse doing office work to earn money for voice lessons. My voice teacher was leaving Syracuse to open a studio in Boston, and I had decided to go to Boston, too, get a job there and continue studying with Mrs. Burnham.

I was not under the illusion that I had a wonderful voice, but I loved singing above everything else, and I wanted to see how far I could go by working hard, making sacrifices if necessary. Singing had become a dominating interest in my life. But because the whole venture was doubtful at best, I was not without some misgivings as to the wisdom of my decision. There seemed to be no harm in trying, however, and I would at least be earning a living. As for the more distant future, I would cross that bridge when I came to it.

Before leaving for Boston, I very much wanted to visit the Adirondacks. I did not expect to resume voice study until fall, and there was consequently no need to go to New England immediately. I began to give serious thought to finding a job so that I might spend the entire summer in the Adirondacks. When someone told me about the Twitchell Lake Inn, I wasted no time in applying there for office work. On receiving word that my application had been accepted, I packed my bags, left Syracuse and on an afternoon early in June 1922, I stepped off the train at Big Moose Station.

The man who came out to meet the train had to get a crate of eggs that had been shipped from Remsen. He also had to go across to the post office for the afternoon mail. Then, with the one passenger, I was the only one going to the Inn, and the rest of the load deposited in the horse-drawn carriage, we started on the three-mile drive to the Inn at Twitchell Lake.

Until the beginning of that summer of 1922, before Sumner Covey and his wife Maude assumed responsibility for the management of the Inn, Earl's daughter Mildred was taking care of the correspondence. She occasionally consulted Earl for advice in answering inquiries about rates and accommodations. Earl was hard at work getting Knoll Cottage ready for guests due to arrive July 1. He was gone all day. In order to get a few minutes of his time, one had to see him before or after meals. Sometimes he would go to the office. At other times Mildred or I, letter in hand, would waylay him for a moment of his attention as he stopped in the kitchen on his way back to work. He did not allow such matters to detain him for long.

When he did stop — in the kitchen, for example — he would take the letter, find a place to sit and in the midst of mealtime activity read the sheet given for his consideration, apparently undisturbed by the hustle and bustle all about him. The first thing that impressed me about Earl was his composure, his look of serenity as he looked down at the letter in his hand.

During the summer the family and employees ate at a long table in the laundry. In his place at the head of the table Earl listened as the men addressed most of their conversation to him. He was a good listener. Amidst the chatter of that heterogeneous group of waitresses, chambermaids and workers about the place, he said little. Now and then with a smile and a twinkle he would make some jesting remark. That was all. Even when Belle the cook brought him his favorite dessert, strawberry shortcake heaped high with berries in a soup plate, even then Earl said little at the table. He smiled his thanks as he accepted the delicious treat. Then afterward as he passed through the kitchen he let Belle know how good her shortcake had tasted.

Knoll Cottage was nearly finished. It was named from its location, on high ground somewhat apart from the main house and the other cottages. In this and in Cliff, the other new cottage, Earl had once again made effective use of birch paneling to finish the inside, while large windows afforded views of the beauty without.

In its final stage of construction, Knoll was the center of interest, and nearly everyone at the Inn had seen it. Busy at my job, I had not taken time to go that far from the main house. Then, too, after one experience with black flies, which left me looking, as someone remarked, like a speckled trout, I decided to stay indoors until the wretched flies were gone.

There would be time later to see the cottage. One day to my surprise Earl asked me if I had been up to see Knoll. Soon after that I made a point of doing so. Earl was busy at the railing of the stairway as I appeared, and while I stood admiring its slender logs of peeled spruce being fitted in place, he looked up and jokingly remarked, "It was growing in the woods this morning."

In order for Earl to take a tree from the woods that morning, draw it in, strip off the bark, shave it smooth and fit it carefully into place, he had to make every move, every minute count. The builder had to know just what to do and just how to do it. Moreover, when Earl was the builder, any work done, even under pressure, had to be done right. When the guests arrived on July 1, the cottage was ready. The completion of Knoll Cottage was the last of Earl's building at the Inn.

Occasionally when he drove out on an errand Earl asked me to accompany him. After selling meat, milk and eggs all day long, I welcomed a quiet evening drive. In the beginning I attributed his invitations to the fact that as I was somewhat older than most of the employees, I might have been a more congenial companion. I saw nothing more than that in Earl's interest in me. Consequently it came as a great surprise when later in the summer he made a proposal of marriage.

When I replied that I was not suited to that life of hard work, he said I "need not worry about the work." How could he say that?

What woman of his acquaintance in the resort business in that part of the woods knew it as anything but a life of hard work, from start to finish? I did not attempt to argue the point. However, I told him that I was sure he would find someone else who would mean as much to him and would make him much happier than I could. Unimpressed he said that he had had "other chances." I still did not see how I could seriously consider his proposal. He said once, with a catch in his voice, "You will probably go to Boston and forget all about us."

But the indecision was not all mine; Earl had had his moments as well. Before proposing to me he had sought the counsel of a long-time guest and friend, Mrs. Clarke, wife of Dr. William Bours Clarke, then rector of Trinity Episcopal Church at Seneca Falls, New York. Her friendship with him, dating back to the early years at Twitchell and her contacts with many and all kinds of people gave Earl great confidence in her judgment. He explained his dilemma: he wanted to propose to me, yet he hesitated to do so on account of the difference in our ages and general background. Mrs. Clarke's answer was prompt and forthright.

"Earl," she said, "there isn't any woman living too good for you. You go right ahead and court her." Mrs. Clarke's encouragement was all Earl needed. He followed her advice.

It was late summer, and I would be leaving Twitchell soon after Labor Day. Earl was waiting for my answer to his proposal. To accept at that time was out of the question. We barely knew each other. Until recently he had only seen me as I sold supplies to the campers, and that had been for only brief intervals when he happened to be around the Inn. After Sumner assumed its management early in the summer I had no direct contact with Earl—until recently when he had taken the initiative in becoming better acquainted with me. Earl, in his middle forties, had already lived a full life. He was a mature person. He was asking me, considerably younger than he, with more formal education but with much less living to my credit, to marry him.

At about this time, in late August, I received a letter from a friend saying that with a friend of hers she wished to spend Labor Day weekend at the Inn. When in the course of conversation Earl learned that friends of mine were arriving as guests, he said, "I want to give them a good time." After they arrived he planned a picnic for us at Brown's Tract Pond.

We drove to the lake. Earl took the food from the pack basket and began to prepare the meal. When we offered to help, he gently but firmly brushed us aside and sent us down to the shore of the lake where we could sit and enjoy its beauty. In a short time everything was ready. We were called to a dinner of fried chicken and browned potatoes cooked to a turn over the open fire. Through it all Earl talked little, but he knew my friends were enjoying the picnic. I was having a good time, too, as good a time, that is, as one could have in my then uncertain state of mind.

With the coming of Labor Day my services at the Inn were no longer needed. I was getting ready to leave when there came an unexpected invitation from Beatrice Noble. She explained that she wished to remain in camp awhile after her parents left and, not wanting to stay alone, asked me to join her. I was reluctant to leave Twitchell; it was so beautiful, especially now, as it began to appear in the glory of its autumn color. And I had not yet given an answer to Earl's proposal. I accepted Beatrice's invitation.

Neither of us will ever forget the picnics and the trips Earl planned for us that fall: to Shallow Lake, reached by trail from one of the Brown's Tract ponds and to Pleasant Lake, a short train ride from Big Moose. At Pleasant Lake there was some land he wanted to see, and Beatrice and I were invited to accompany him. He had arranged with Mrs. Iva Denio, living at the Station, to have dinner ready for us at her home on our return that evening. I can still remember the fried chicken, home-made rolls and cake she served us. Earl's thoughtful provision made a perfect ending to our day.

Nor shall we ever forget those warm September days when we transplanted small evergreens and canoed down the lake for mail and supplies nor the sunlit hours on Beatrice's porch, when the peace and beauty that was Twitchell entered into and became part of us. That will remain with us always.

It was possible in such a place as this to see our situation, Earl's and mine, in clearer perspective. Even so this decision, which was to affect us both for the rest of our lives, had to be based solely on what

I had been able to see and learn of him in one short summer. The seemingly sensible course would have been to tell him as kindly as possible that I could not accept his proposal, thus ending the matter then and there.

But somehow I could not do that to Earl Covey. Impressed by the love and respect accorded him by the entire Twitchell community, I knew well that in recent years he had been through deep sorrow and that he felt lost and alone. Certainly under these circumstances his proposal was not to be treated lightly.

There was another and very important factor in the situation: as a member of his summer household I had seen Earl in his home, his own environment, with his family and others in close association with him. I had seen him in those contacts and experiences of day-to-day living, which reveal a person's true character. I had been able to see the real Earl Covey. Not once in that entire summer did I see him when he appeared ruffled or impatient. Quiet and gentle always, ready to help or advise when asked, friendly, approachable, yet keeping modestly in the background when his presence was not required — such was my early impression of him. Further acquaintance with him confirmed that impression.

When telling me of his love he was simple, direct and sincere. Probably no courtship was ever conducted in fewer words. But so sweet, so kind, so eager was he in his efforts to please that what he did was more eloquent than many words would have been. In this endearing way Earl gradually won me over. I had intended to go to Boston in the fall. But this man whom I had learned to love changed my mind. When it came time for Beatrice to close camp in October, I told Earl that I would marry him.

Before we left Twitchell that fall it was getting cold. In fact, there had been a light snow fall. One day when Earl took us for a drive I was trying to wrap myself in the car blanket to keep warm. Finally Earl stopped at a place along the way, went in and after a few minutes returned with a safety pin with which to secure the blanket. Then I was comfortable.

On one of my last days in camp Earl brought a jeweler's card to obtain my ring size. He asked, "Do you want a ring now or wait for the real thing?" He gave emphasis as he spoke to "the real thing."

Assuming that he referred to a wedding ring, I told him I would wait. I never cared about wearing rings and that there might not be an engagement ring did not trouble me in the least.

I decided to visit a friend in Sherwood, New York, before returning to New England. Earl offered to take me in the car, and so we made the trip together. He dreaded the drive back alone, but we parted with the understanding that he would spend Christmas at my home in Stafford Springs, Connecticut and meet my parents. Just before leaving Twitchell I received my first gift from Earl, a brown handbag containing one hundred dollars. I wonder if he knew how little money I had at that time?

Mother and Father received without comment the news about Earl and our desire to be married. That he had spent most of his life in the woods, had worked hard and had done a great deal of building was not particularly exciting. That he was a very fine, highly respected man could not have greatly impressed them. Knowing nothing more than I was able to tell about him, they could form little idea of the kind of person he was.

That I, a college graduate, should wish to marry a man of limited formal education who was thirteen years my senior and whose children were grown up and married — a man who had lived practically all his life in the woods and would probably want to remain there — must have caused my parents considerable misgiving. There was nothing for them to do but wait and see what this man was like.

Earl came to Stafford for Christmas as planned. It was a brief visit because he had started building a house at the Station, which he wanted to finish by spring, and there were still months of work to be done before it would be ready. I well remember the first evening he was with us. After the preliminary visiting and getting acquainted, Earl turned his chair to face my parents directly and then told them why he had come.

"I would like her to share the future with me," he said. For a moment no one said a word. Mother was the first to speak. "But she can't do that work."

"She won't have to worry about the work," Earl assured her. She had nothing more to say. From then on, Father continued the conversation. He liked Earl from the beginning, and it was not long before the two men became warm friends. Before the evening was over Father was willing to give his consent to our marriage. Mother acquiesced.

In speaking of work, Mother meant the resort business. As a matter of fact, at the time of Earl's first visit to Stafford there was no resort in view. Then he told us what had happened after I left Twitchell in the fall.

Henry Covey, now past the age when he could continue his business, had decided to sell Camp Crag. As soon as Earl learned this he made his father an offer, which had been tentatively accepted. Just then someone else heard that the property was for sale and offered a higher price. Henry decided to accept the higher offer. Earl made a trip to Queer Lake one night to explain to this man his side of the situation. The final decision rested with Henry Covey. It must have been a difficult one for him to make, with the desire of his own son on the one hand and the more tempting offer on the other. Business had declined in recent years, and Henry had lost money. The other man got the place. To lose Camp Crag with all its exciting possibilities for development, when he almost had it, was a bitter blow to Earl.

That was the story Earl told us when he came to Stafford for Christmas. From then on Camp Crag became private property, was later resold and developed into smaller camp sites. Earl's disappointment over the loss of that beautiful spot remained with him as long as he lived.

But there was no time for brooding. Camp Crag was definitely out of the picture, and there was a house at Big Moose Station to be finished by spring. Before Earl left we agreed to wait until we knew when the house would be ready before setting the date for the wedding.

Second Marriage

Late in January the local paper carried an announcement of our engagement, and I began to plan for a spring wedding. Earl had told me it would not be necessary for me to provide anything for the house, that it would be completely furnished. With part of the money he had given me, I purchased some table linen and a few place settings of silverware. That was all.

In March, Earl wrote that we could plan for a wedding in April, and so the fourteenth was set as the date. As busy as he was during the early part of 1923, he wrote frequently. He even took time to make snapshots to enclose with his letters, showing the little house as it neared completion.

One day a small package arrived in the mail. It was my engagement ring. Earl afterward explained why it was so long coming. When he specified in his order to the jeweler that the ring was to have a perfect stone, he was told that he might have to wait. I was accordingly given my choice while at Twitchell — an engagement ring such as he could have given me at that time, or "the real thing," which would come later.

An engagement ring is something very special. I realize this now, as I had not before. When I saw my ring I was glad that I had waited for "the real thing." Its perfect diamond represented to me the very best that was in Earl's power to give.

By the first week in April plans for the home wedding were complete. It was to be very simple, with just a few of our friends and neighbors. Earl arrived early in the week for the wedding, which was to take place on Saturday. That he had finished the house with a few days to spare was remarkable, in view of the fact that just before leaving Big Moose he had negotiated with his father for the purchase of about sixty-six acres of land on the South Bay shore of the lake. And this at the time he was finishing and furnishing our house, to be all ready for us on our return from the wedding trip.

It had all happened so recently and he had been so busy that he had not had time to write about it before coming. Perhaps, too, he preferred to deliver this important news in person rather than by letter.

For months Earl had been looking for Adirondack property that he could develop into a resort. He had given up his earlier plan of going to California. There was land at Pleasant Lake for sale, and he had planned the trip to see the place, inviting Beatrice Noble and me to go with him. But the Pleasant Lake property was not what he wanted. Then there was the bright though brief prospect of acquiring Camp Crag, finally there came the purchase on South Bay.

Father, from his lean height of six feet three inches, smiled down at Earl as they stood talking together about the property. "What are you going to do with it?" he asked.

Earl, looking up, replied, "Oh, build something on it."

To one who knew them both, this brief exchange highlighted the two men as they stood facing each other. Father, the cautious, conservative New Englander; Earl with his pioneer spirit, ready for the next venture, confident in his ability to accomplish whatever task he set out to do. They were very different, these two. Yet in their gentler qualities they were alike. Both were modest, kindly and tolerant, and it was easy for them to meet on common ground. They understood each other. They spoke the same language.

Mother, meanwhile, was reserving her judgment about Earl. Since they had first met, she had said little either to him or about him. As a rule she expressed her opinions plainly, and she was a person of positive opinions. The silence on her part was unusual. Having always laid great stress on the correct use of English, she was quick to correct errors of speech by members of the family. Her one comment during Earl's Christmas visit was this: "He speaks so low that if he does make a mistake no one knows it."

When he came for the wedding Mother was still reserving judgment. But at least she had no criticism to make. Earl fitted into the plans and activities of that busy week so easily and so quietly that there was nothing she could criticize. He may have been aware of her coolness, but at no time did he attempt to "make a good impression" or overstep in any way.

One day while I was busy with wedding preparations Mother and my two sisters took Earl for a ride. When they stopped at the house on returning Earl was out and around on Mother's side to assist her out of the car. She looked up, and there he was. How did he get there so quickly? She could not understand it. She spoke of it several times. The unexpected promptness with which Earl had rendered this simple service impressed Mother.

On the afternoon of April 14, 1923 Earl and I were married in the presence of a few Stafford friends. At that time, the town was not easily accessible, and the only guests to come from a distance were our Twitchell friends Dr. and Mrs. Noble. Starting out from New York, they took a train to Hartford. From there to Stafford was a trolley ride of an hour and a half. It was wonderfully kind of them to make the long and tedious trip, but they were willing to do it for Earl Covey. I feel sure that during the informal reception following the ceremony they expressed to my friends their high regard for this man from the Adirondacks who was marrying into the Alden family.

We left that afternoon for our wedding trip to Washington, where we spent nearly a week sightseeing. In addition to places in the nation's capital, which all visitors like to see, we included spots of particular interest to Earl. We drove past the house where he and Addie had lived and where William was born. We saw the little house he built on land he purchased during the year he was in the city. We took a drive to Georgetown Falls. At the time Earl had lived in Washington, he and his cousin furnished ties for a short railroad line that was being built from there to Georgetown. We saw no railroad in 1923. It had apparently gone out of existence.

After enjoying five days in Washington we were ready to leave for our home at Big Moose. The Nobles invited us to visit them in New York on our way. We accepted their kind invitation and enjoyed their hospitality for a weekend. On Saturday evening they took us to the opera. On Sunday morning we attended a church service, and in the afternoon Mrs. Noble invited a few Twitchell friends in the New York area to tea, which afforded us the opportunity of a visit with them. The weekend was a delightful ending for our wedding trip. On Monday morning we said goodbye to the Noble family and took a train, which arrived at Big Moose Station that afternoon.

Living at the Station

Earl had arranged to have our house ready with everything in place on our arrival, even to dishes, linen and silverware — and all in such good taste. The living room was just the right size. It was beautifully proportioned and, to make it complete, had one of Earl's fireplaces. A wide doorway connected this room with the dining room. In each of these rooms were two large windows. Convenient and well planned throughout, it all seemed as nearly perfect as a home could be.

After unpacking and getting settled Earl lost no time in beginning work on his newly acquired property at Big Moose Lake. For this job he had to have men and horses. He engaged his friend and neighbor, John Denio, to drive the team and found two other men to act as helpers. First they had to build a road from the bridge spanning Big Moose Lake Outlet to the building site. This entailed cutting trees, clearing the ground, removing rocks, grading and filling in. Soon the black-fly season was upon them when none but hardy fishermen and those on necessary business ventured into the woods for more than a few minutes at a time. But Earl could not stop for black flies. The work went on. After finishing the road he started on the buildings. Before long a barn, a garage and living quarters were ready for use.

That was a hard summer both for Earl and for me. Although household tasks had always been part of my upbringing, I had never enjoyed such work, and perhaps because of that I found it physically tiring. However, on marrying I was prepared to accept a certain amount of housework as part of life, as have most other women. What others had done I could do. It was probably fortunate that neither of us could foresee the difficulties that lay ahead.

That first summer for me was one of continual struggle with a wood-burning stove. First, I had to learn to build a fire so that it would not go out. Then I had to learn how it worked when it did burn. If I went away and left it after it was well started, I would find on returning that the wood had all burned, the fire was out and I had to start over again.

If the fire was not built soon enough or did not burn as it should, supper was not always ready when the men came home at night. Earl finally told me that he could not keep his men if the meal was not ready on time.

At one point he was so sorely tried that, lest my feelings be hurt, he cautioned me not to take too seriously anything he might say in a moment of irritation. But not once that summer did he appear visibly impatient or annoyed. He helped when he could. In the morning he cooked a breakfast of bacon, eggs and griddlecakes for his two

A Fresh Start

Margaret Rose Covey died during the summer of 1923 after Earl and Frances were married. Her death was a loss to everyone, but Earl stopped his work and saw to the arrangements for her funeral and burial in Canada.

men and himself. At night he washed the dishes. He once asked if I wanted someone to help with the housework, even though he thought it was not necessary and could not understand why I found my task difficult. Knowing that we would soon be moving to the Lake and that someone else would do the cooking there, I decided to get along without extra help for the remainder of our time at the Station.

A brief incident occurred which, while it has no direct bearing on other events of that first summer, serves to show the outgoing friendliness so characteristic of Earl. We were on our way home from Twitchell late one Sunday afternoon when he saw two men near the store at the Station. Something prompted him to suggest that we take them to the house and give them supper. They did not seem to be in any particular need nor did they appear to be looking for a free meal. To us they were total strangers. To them, we were just two people in a passing car. In my utter amazement it never occurred to me to ask Earl why he would take in those two strange men, just because they were strangers, perhaps. I marveled at his desire to be hospitable but was completely without enthusiasm for the idea. The men ate supper somewhere else.

In addition to his burden of work and responsibility Earl was saddened that summer of 1923 by the death of his stepmother. He stopped his work, made the arrangements for her funeral service and attended to the details of burial at her home in Canada. We accompanied Earl's father to Mother Covey's final resting-place. After that Father Covey stayed on alone at the Rose Cottage, at the turn where one leaves the Eagle Bay road to drive down to the lake. Earl was able to keep in touch with his father as he went back and forth to work.

In five months' time Earl cleared ground, built a road and put up a house to live in. By mid-September we were ready to move from our little house at the Station to the place, which was to be our home at Big Moose Lake for the next fifteen years. The building we occupied, later used as the laundry, had rooms on the second floor, which accommodated the Coveys and the men in Earl's employ.

During the winter, early in 1924, I returned to my home in Connecticut for a visit with my parents. It was the first time I had seen them since my marriage. In that time I was able to gain perspective on the experiences of the months just past. The clearer perspective helped me to become adjusted to the loss of our first child, Elizabeth, who lived only twenty-four hours after her premature birth in October. This occurred soon after we were settled at the lake, probably the result of a ride over the rough road under construction to Eagle Bay. I had not ridden over the road all summer, and, feeling perfectly well, I thought a brief trip on an errand would do no harm. I learned to my sorrow that I should not have gone. Much had happened during that first year of our married life. I felt the need for a change, a fresh outlook.

Chapter IV

Henry Covey

After a two-week visit in Stafford I returned to Big Moose to discover that in the meantime Earl had moved again, this time to the Rose Cottage. His father, no longer able to withstand the rigors of a long winter alone, needed someone with him. It was so clearly the right thing for Earl to do that I did not for a moment question his decision. Earl's place was with his father, and it was a comfort to the frail and lonely man to have his son there.

Henry Covey was among the first to settle permanently at Big Moose Lake. That was in 1888. In the nearly thirty-five years he was at Camp Crag he had seen the lake develop from little more than a wilderness to a popular vacation spot. His own camp had grown from a small place for hunting and fishing parties to a successful summer resort. He had gone to the woods at a time when he had to be able to do everything himself, from cooking a meal to shoeing a horse. Self-reliant and resourceful, he had met and overcome the obstacles, which were a part of life in what was then a primitive out-of-the-way part of New York State.

All supplies for Crag Point were transported by boat, sometimes by the "Pickle Boat" from the Glenmore Hotel, sometimes by one of Covey's from Henry's boat landing in South Bay. There was no road to Camp Crag. Henry would not have one. Nothing was allowed to disturb his guests. The Pickle Boat, when delivering supplies to campers on the lake, was not permitted to blow its whistle when passing the Point.

The host of Camp Crag was particular, moreover, about his guests, and anyone of whom he did not approve did not stay long. On the other hand he would go to great lengths to please those he liked. He worked without thought of sparing himself, and he expected his employees to do the same. If they did not, or if they incurred his displeasure in any way, they received from him a tongue-lashing, which they did not soon forget. His keen wit and homely philosophy born of his years in the woods won for him warm friends among guests who returned from year to year to enjoy not only the beauty and the quiet of Camp Crag but also the unique and individual personality of Henry Covey.

The years after World War I brought many changes. With the coming of the automobile people were going to vacation places accessible by roads over which they could drive their own cars. Fewer were making long stays in any one place. Spending a night here, a night there, then driving on, was becoming the practice of visitors to vacation spots everywhere. This was beginning to affect places that, like Camp Crag, were off the beaten track.

Another and more important reason for the decline of business at Camp Crag was the fact that Father and Mother Covey were no longer young. It was increasingly difficult for them to do the work necessary to keep the place going. And so in 1922 they sold the property, and the aging couple moved to the Rose Cottage, originally built for Grandma and Grandpa Rose who occupied it during their last years. Grandpa Rose was Mother Covey's brother. By the following spring Mother Covey's health was failing. She lived until July. After her death Father Covey stayed alone at Rose Cottage. When we moved to the lake Earl tried to persuade him to leave the house at the top of the hill. It was perhaps just as well that he did not. Rose Cottage, built for winter living, was more comfortable than the house at the lake would have been.

Our going to the Rose Cottage made it possible for Earl's father to remain a while longer in the house that had become his home. He spent some of the time at his desk and some of the time at simple tasks around the house. At other times he sat by the window where he could see the occasional passers-by. Once in a while, when looking for something he could not find, or encountering a new and unfamiliar way of doing something, he would just say, in patient resignation, "It doesn't matter."

Perhaps it did not matter. Once a vigorous man with positive opinions, he had learned to accept uncomplainingly situations beyond his power to change or control. But it was a sad reminder that his active years were past, his work nearly done. The best part of his day was when Earl came home at night. After supper we would sit in the kitchen while he and Earl discussed events of interest or the building down by the lake, which Father Covey followed with great interest. He frequently expressed ideas of his own regarding the work.

With the coming of spring Father Covey showed signs of failing strength. Even so, he got out his fishing rod now and then and walked down the hill to the outlet to try his luck. When he could land a trout he found the effort worthwhile, but he was much disgusted when nothing but a sucker rose to his bait. He complained little of not feeling well. Apparently neither he nor Earl thought it necessary to consult a physician. He welcomed the visits of friends and neighbors who called occasionally to see him.

One day the arrival of an elderly man surprised and delighted both Earl and his father. He was Fred Hess, formerly a guide, builder and hotel man at Inlet on Fourth Lake. He accompanied Earl on a hunting trip to Maine some years before, and they had not seen each other for a long time. Invited to remain for a visit, Fred spent several days at the Rose Cottage, going from there to visit people in the vicinity. With no other means of transportation he was obliged to walk.

While the men were sitting outside one mild evening, Earl, seeing that Fred was footsore after hours of walking, suggested that Fred remove his shoes and socks. Earl, meanwhile, went inside, returned with soap, towel and a basin of water, and while the older man sat resting on the porch Earl bathed his feet. Shortly afterward Fred Hess went on his way. We did not see him again.

By the spring of 1924 the first guest cottage of our new resort was nearing completion. We planned to occupy it ourselves until the main house was finished. I was eagerly looking forward to being in our own home again. Earl's anticipation was doubtless tempered by some apprehension lest his father would decide not to go with us. That Father Covey did not wish to leave Rose Cottage was evident whenever the matter was mentioned. We could only wait and see what would happen.

Finally the day came when Earl said, hoping against hope that Father Covey would consent. We were ready to move. He was asking his father to leave Rose Cottage for a place that was not home to the aging man and never would be really. Hardly daring to look, I turned to see what Father Covey's response would be. Never shall I forget that frail, pathetic figure as he faced his son.

"Earl," he said, "I am in your hands. I will do whatever you say."

It did not take us long to move and get settled in the new house. We named it after Father Covey. It still retains the name Henry Covey Cottage. With his father's comfort in mind, Earl had provided for him a bedroom and bath downstairs. His desk was in the living room near the large front window from which he could turn in his swivel chair and look across South Bay. From a window to the west he could see the main house under construction, a sight always of interest to him. But there was a sad, faraway look in his brown eyes. Now and then, his mind not entirely clear, he spoke as though he were back at Camp Crag, talking to someone there. Through the summer until early September he was up and around the house. From then on he did not feel able to leave his room.

On the night of October 11 Earl decided to remain at his father's bedside. He watched through the night. Once his father attempted to tell him something, which Earl tried to understand but could not. At least the dying man knew that his son was there with him. About five o'clock Earl came upstairs to let me know that he thought the end was near. It was not long.

As we stood beside him early on the morning of October 12, 1924, Father Covey's spirit quietly slipped away finally released from its burden of weakness and earthly care.

Henry H. Covey was laid to rest in the family lot in the Forest Hills Cemetery in Utica. I asked Earl at the time if his mother's remains could not be brought and placed beside those of his father. Earl replied in a choked voice that he had been unable to find anything that could have been removed from her grave in the cemetery at Beeches Bridge. Had it been possible he would have provided a place for her beside his father.

Chapter V

Covewood

Building the Main House

It was mid October. The work of the winter ahead depended on closing in the sides and getting a roof on the main building in the next two months. It was a race with time. The last roof board was nailed down just before snow came. There was never, so far as I know, any plan for the first floor on paper. The plan was fairly simple, the front part consisting of living and dining rooms with a wide hall between. Behind these were the kitchen, a small dining room and cupboards and pantry. For the second floor, in order to determine the exact location of baths and clothes closets, there was a plan drawn on brown wrapping paper. Ten of the eleven sleeping rooms had private baths. When Earl knew where these were to be, he had no further need for the plan on paper. I saw it just once.

During the winter's work on the new building there was one interruption — the ice job. Before the days of electric refrigeration, ice houses and coolers were filled with ice cut from the lake. For this there was no set time scheduled on the calendar. It was done when the ice was ready to cut, often in sub-zero temperatures with a bitter wind blowing. For about four days it took every able-bodied man on the place with perhaps an extra one or two to help. There had to be hot food and plenty of it ready when the men came in to eat. It took good horses as well. All day long the ice, cut into cakes, was moved out of the water onto the horse-drawn sled. As soon as there was a load, the horses, Bill and Dan, with all they could draw, started off the ice. At a signal from the teamster, with a quick rush up the bank, the team strained as they pulled the sled onto dry ground. It had to be done quickly. Once under motion there was no stopping the horses until their load was safely on shore, to be hauled on to the cooler. For four days, all day long, this went on. When the last cake was shoved into place, covered with sawdust and the door of the big ice chamber closed tightly for another year, everyone breathed easier. Perhaps Bill and Dan did, too.

With the ice job out of the way, Earl was free again to concentrate on the main house. The roughing in of the plumbing, installing the water pipes between floors and partitions, was done. It took a plumber's full time for several weeks.

The fireplaces, three of them, were next. Earl began with the one in the living room, the most difficult of the three, which was to be cut from that hardest of materials, Adirondack granite. It took a month to cut and lay the stone for that fireplace. Each piece had to be just the right size and shape to fit into its place. Earl would have a stone almost ready to lay in place when it would break the wrong way, and with a fresh piece he would start over again. It seemed as though he would never reach the mantel stone.

But he did. One day, coming to see how the fireplace was progressing, I stepped into the room just as that mantel was being raised into position. It was like being at the setting of a cornerstone. To be sure, there were still days of work ahead. The fireplace was built to the ceiling, but once the mantel was in place the longest and hardest part of the work was done.

The way the fireplace fits into its place in the living room with dignity and simplicity of design, in the artistry with which the rose-colored pieces are combined with the gray, in its workmanship, so fine that not a tool mark shows, it stands as a monument to its builder. To one who saw that fireplace in the making, it is more than just a monument. It is something of Earl Covey himself.

The dining-room fireplace, of broken stone, with just enough cutting to fit the pieces together, did not take long.

The fireplace in the hall was built of cobblestone. From the floor to the mantel it did not greatly differ from others of similar construction, but a large round stone above its mantel attracted immediate attention, and many people asked, "Where did you get that

The living room at Covewood featured one of the Covey signature fireplaces facing the lake. All the wood finishes are natural, and the details are true to an Adirondack style that is copied into the 21st century.

stone?"

With a twinkle, Earl would reply, "Oh, up by the road."

In its size, about twenty-two inches in diameter, and its shape, as round as a natural stone could be, Earl had seen its possibilities. He brought it down and built it into his fireplace. One day after we had moved into the main house Earl appeared at the desk in the hall with something in his hand. Placing it on the desk he said, "Don't throw that away." Without further comment, he walked on. It was an exact miniature of the big round stone in the hall fireplace. From that time the small stone was a paperweight on the office desk. It remains as a cherished souvenir on the mantel of a family fireplace.

After the fireplaces the finishing proceeded without difficulty. In addition to private baths, four of the front rooms upstairs had balcony porches. Construction of the guestrooms was not rustic, but with walls tinted in a light shade they were pleasant and restful.

Covewood

DINING ROOM AT COVEWOOD, BIG MOOSE, N.Y.

The Covewood dining room was where guests would all gather at the end of the day. It was a comfortable place with good food served from the kitchen by the summer help, and families would find familiar faces returning from one year to the next.

Rooms downstairs took longer. The ceiling beams, the arch over the entrance between hall and living room and the front-stair railing were all of peeled spruce logs. These were stripped of their bark, cut and planed to proper size, then sandpapered and polished by hand. The big living room was a good place for this work. At times the shavings from planing were knee-deep on the floor.

It was a hard job to get the ceiling beams into place. The beams had to be raised from staging and held overhead until they could be fitted into grooves chiseled out to receive them at each end. Earl finished many a day's work with an aching neck.

The sidewalls, paneled in birch, went on much more easily. Linseed oil, followed by polishing, brought out the rich warm tint of the native wood. The floors were finished last.

In finishing the exterior, Earl used spruce slabs instead of the half-logs like those that his father had used at Camp Crag and those

One of Earl Covey's guests said to his host, "All that you have done before has been in preparation for this." Covewood was the result of Covey's experience at Twitchell Lake, at a camp built in Canada and his work on the memorial bridge for his son William who died in the Army.

that he had used himself at the Inn at Twitchell. Otherwise the general woodsy appearance of our new home was much the same as the other two places. Large cedar posts supported the verandah roof. Steps of stone, adding strength and beauty, completed the entrance to the building.

Approaching the bridge across the outlet to Big Moose Lake, one glimpses a curve in the shoreline just before the waters of South Bay enter the stream that flows under the bridge. From that little cove and from Earl's family name we adopted the name for our resort, "Covewood."

Contact With Guests and Employees

On July 4, 1925, in a pouring rainstorm, we moved from the Henry Covey Cottage to the main house. Our first guests arrived a

The verandah at Covewood gives a spectacular view out into Big Moose Lake. Comfortable chairs line the wall and often are moved to capture the sunlight or the shade where guests have spent afternoons absorbing the wonder of the Adirondacks and her sparkling lakes.

few days later. Some had been visitors at the lake while Covewood was under construction and decided they would like to try the new place. They came with a few of their friends. Others appeared, as the word got around about Earl Covey's Inn at Big Moose Lake. There was very little printed advertising for the first summer. In fact, a considerable number of our people over the years came simply on the recommendation of those who had been guests themselves at Covewood.

And not only house guests came. There were sightseers, scores of them, that summer and summers thereafter. Everyone who had heard of the new place wanted to see it. They admired the spacious rooms, fireplaces, picture windows, private baths, balcony porches. They marveled at the large peeled log arching over the wide entrance between the living room and the front hall. Was that a natural curve? At the foot of the stairs the round spruce railing curved into

Covewood, like most of Adirondack hotels, catered to sportsmen. Builder and innkeeper Earl Covey (at left) knew the woods like the back of his hand, and this party like many others reaped the bounty of his experience and familiarity with the area.

the newel posts on either side. How did he find two trees of the same size with the same curve? Did they really grow that way? To which Earl would jokingly reply, "The woods are full of crooks."

Among our first visitors after the opening of Covewood were our Twitchell friends, the Nobles. Dr. Noble, in company with his family, walked through the rooms downstairs noting details silently as he looked around. He did the same upstairs still without saying a word.

Earl stood at the desk in the front hall as we came downstairs. Greetings were exchanged, and for the first time Dr. Noble spoke. "Earl," he began. There was a pause. Then Dr. Noble continued, "All that you have done before has been in preparation for this."

All that he had done before … When Earl began to build at Twitchell there was no road, only a rough trail to the lake. Slowly the Inn came into being, first the main house, then cottages, one by one.

Covewood

Earl Covey prided himself on taking care of his guests. He saw to it that people staying at Covewood had good food and good beds. No one who attended his square dances or his outdoor suppers would forget them. His steaks cooked over the open fire behind the Inn were legendary.

In addition to his own work, he built cottages for others around the lake. He built a camp in Canada and finally, at the outlet of Twitchell Lake, the bridge as a memorial to William.

At no time during his building at Twitchell was Earl consciously preparing for a specific future task. He was merely doing the work at hand as faithfully and as well as he knew how, and the experience he gained made possible this new place at Big Moose Lake. Dr. Noble, however, could look back to the beginning of Earl's career, to the years when the builder was developing and improving his skill. In this latest achievement the doctor could see the total result of all that Earl had learned, all that he had done, in the past. The Twitchell years had in many ways prepared him for the building of Covewood.

We opened for the summer of 1925 with the main house and the Henry Covey Cottage. During the next three years Earl added four more cottages, which kept him busy building. His primary contacts with the guests were on occasions such as the outdoor suppers, when he took charge of broiling the steak. As suppertime approached guests gathered and watched. Unperturbed by the activity around him, Earl worked quietly, easily, tending steaks that were on the grate over a bed of hot coals. Then quick words from the master cook, "All ready!" And everyone sat down at a long table to an outdoor meal planned around porterhouse steak, broiled and served from the open fire.

Another contact with the guests, which Earl enjoyed perhaps even more than the suppers, was the square dances. Long a tradition at Twitchell, they became part of the life at Covewood. Barney Lepper, the Big Moose Station agent, came occasionally to call the changes in the dancing. Otherwise Earl did it himself, sometimes calling and dancing at the same time. At country-dances the callers would dance if they felt like it, and it did not interfere with their calling.

There was no fixed charge for the dances. During the evening someone would pass the hat for contributions, and if there were not enough to pay for the music Earl would make up the difference from his own pocket. During the pause between dances Earl visited with guests. Then at the call, "Four more couples!" the dancing started again.

During the regular intermission he was in the kitchen dishing up ice cream. Some of the young people took this on trays to guests waiting for refreshments in the living room, in the front hall, on the stairs, on the verandah outside and wherever they could find places to sit. Following the intermission there were one or two more dances before the party came to an end. After the last dancer had gone and the place was quiet once more, Earl would say, "I think they had a good time." He knew they had had a good time. They told him so as they bid him good night.

Any situation that had in it the element of surprise appealed to Earl. One day in July the elder Dr. and Mrs. Herben came from their camp at Twitchell to have dinner at Covewood. It was a year when the snow had remained in shaded spots long after winter had past. Before dinner the Herbens asked Earl if they might have two or three small trees to take back to Twitchell that afternoon. Earl agreed to have the trees ready.

After their dinner the Herbens came out of the dining room expecting to find the trees at the desk. The trees were not there, and they started away empty-handed. As they approached the Covewood bridge on their way they came to the wagon road leading to the sawmill. There beside the road were the trees, their tips just showing above a pile of snow. And there stood Earl, waiting to present the trees to the Herbens. Not for anything would he have missed seeing their delight as they gratefully accepted the surprise he had in store for them.

That same summer Earl provided some Fourth of July guests with a pan of snow for "jackwax," the popular "maple sugar on snow" usually enjoyed in the early spring sugaring-off season. The guests enjoyed celebrating the glorious Fourth in this unique fashion but no more than Earl did himself in providing something totally unexpected.

Building and maintenance of the property kept Earl busy most of the time. Only on rare occasions did he concern himself with housekeeping matters. That was the women's realm.

He did not hesitate to step in, however, if he thought the situation called for his action, such as the time one summer when the waitresses had been unhappy for one reason or another. Little was said openly, but one could sense an undercurrent of their dissatisfaction.

Finally, one evening after their work was done, they were complaining to me about something they did not like. While I was trying to straighten out the difficulty, Earl suddenly appeared in the doorway. No one knew that he was in the next room where he could hear the entire conversation. Before anyone else could speak, he said to the girls, "You're fired!"

His tone, his manner left nothing for them to do but walk out, in shocked silence. They left Covewood the next day. I went to bed that night not knowing who would serve breakfast to guests the next morning. I could only trust that somehow Earl would see us through, and he did. By breakfast time he had rounded up enough local help to tide us over until we could replace the discharged waitresses.

Even though busy with his own tasks, Earl was aware of what was going on around him, and he was quick to express his opinion on matters that were not to his liking. One thing of which he heartily disapproved was late hours the employees kept after their day's work was done. On one occasion he was returning to Covewood late in the evening as some of the girls were coming in. He directed the boyfriends accompanying them to leave at once. The boys did so and disappeared down the road. Instead of immediately going on to the main house, Earl waited to see what would happen. In a few minutes the boyfriends reappeared. To their surprise Earl was there to meet them. When he told them to leave the second time, the boys did not come back that night.

During our early years at Covewood the prevailing wage for dining room and chamber work was a dollar a day plus room and board. One chambermaid, after working awhile, expressed some dissatisfaction with her wages to Earl. To be sure, they seem now ridiculously low, but at that time today's wages were undreamed of. Moreover, then as now, it was understood at the outset what the employer would pay the employee for the service rendered. Earl listened to what Mrs. J. had to say, and then he asked, "Are you overworked?"

He knew she was not being overworked, which she herself had to admit in answer to his question. There was nothing further to be said, nor was there any increase in her wages. The matter was settled just as quietly and definitely as that.

On the other hand Earl was ready to pay well for proven ability, as in the case of our cook, Belle Nolett. For several years our experience with cooks had been varied, at times unsatisfactory. Good cooks were hard to find. We had one very fine pastry cook, Mrs. Ada Brownell, whose cakes and pies saved the situation when the meat and vegetable cooking all but ruined the Covewood reputation. Even for a small place like ours, we had to have two cooks when it was impossible to find one who would do both meat and pastry. How we wished we could have Belle. She had worked for the Coveys at Twitchell in the past and would do all the cooking. She had recently been working near New York City, and there seemed little chance of having her at Covewood. One day someone told us that Belle had come to Utica to live and at the time was not working. We learned her Utica address and wasted no time in going to see her.

It had been several years since we had last seen Belle. She listened with interest as Earl gave her news about the family and Twitchell people that she knew. After they had talked for what seemed to me a long time, Earl came to the point and explained the reason for our coming. We needed a cook and wanted her for the job. Belle apparently liked the idea and agreed. With that settled she and Earl resumed conversation on other matters, and we went on visiting a while longer. Nothing had been said about wages or anything else in connection with the job. I realized afterward that Belle already knew the Coveys and the Covey ways. She knew her job and what would be expected of her. She did not have to be told.

Finally Earl decided it was time to leave. Almost casually he said to Belle, "Set your price." No quibbling, no bickering. Belle knew that she would receive what she asked. Earl was confident that what she asked would be reasonable, and that, after all, was all that mattered. From then on our cooking worries were over. In addition to her exceptional ability as a cook, Belle was clean, economical and always mindful of our best interests. She was a wonderful person to work with. The highest-paid employee on our staff, she earned every cent she received. She was like a member of our family, and we kept in touch with her as long as she lived.

Within three years from the time we opened for business, four more cottages were added. These, in addition to the main house and the Henry Covey Cottage, comprised Covewood's guest accommodations. By this time others were calling on Earl for building work, and he was away from Covewood much of the time. I once asked him which he liked better, hotel work or building.

"I like to take care of people," he replied. He did like taking care of people. He saw to it that his guests had good food and good beds. He liked giving them a good time. No one who attended his square dances or his outdoor suppers will ever forget them. But he had a resourceful and creative mind. Each building job with its own possibilities and its unique problems challenged his skill and his imagination. Always willing to learn, ever open to new ideas and new ways of doing things, Earl found that building was more than just a job. It had become an absorbing interest. Not that he liked taking care of people any less — he just liked building a little bit more. Then, too, another and important factor was the additional income from the extra work. When resort business suffered during the Great Depression, it was Earl's outside building that kept us going. Had it not been for that, we might have lost everything.

Accidents

Work in the woods has its own hazards. Earl never had a serious accident while felling trees, although he did have some hairbreadth escapes. One time a branch he was holding as it was being sawed from the tree trunk suddenly sprang back into the air, carrying him with it. He must have known a few breathless moments as, suspended in mid-air, he clung to the branch. Fortunately the branch was strong enough to hold Earl's weight until he could lower himself to the ground in safety.

One winter's day as Earl was clearing snow from the porch roof of the Henry Covey Cottage the pile in front of him gave way and slid off the roof. Unable to hold himself back, Earl fell down after it and landed on the ground below. It was a drop of fifteen feet.

Hearing his call for help I rushed out to find him in a snowbank unable to move. One of his men was near by, and the two of us helped him to the house. He was in pain, and I wanted to call a doctor immediately.

"Now, just a minute, just a minute!" were his first words, calling for a chair so that he could sit down and decide what to do next—and he would be the one to decide. The doctor was not to be called, but there was no more snow shoveling that afternoon.

The next morning, after a sleepless night because of the pain, he changed his mind and decided to see the doctor. The examination disclosed two fractured ribs, which had to be bound with adhesive tape. In the days that followed the itching from the tight bandage was almost unbearable, worse than the pain of the fracture. Once the bones had knit and the bandage removed, however, Earl was none the worse for his experience.

One story I often heard was of the time on a building job when Earl called to one of his men on the roof to throw down a hammer. The hammer had been left on the roof. It was a good-sized hammer. The man hesitated. Earl, not wishing to be kept waiting, again exclaimed somewhat impatiently, "Throw it. Throw it!"

The man threw it. It struck Earl, and it hit hard.

"Well," said Earl, laughing as he recovered from the blow, "I asked for it, and I got it."

The nearest Earl came to having a serious accident was with his truck. He was driving down the old Kingsford hill with a heavy load one afternoon when something happened to the truck's clutch. He could not shift into low gear and then found that he could not use the brake. The only course left was to try to keep the truck on the road. Fortunately no other cars were coming. He was able to continue on until he reached the turn at the foot of the hill. By that time the truck was going too fast to make the curve. The loaded truck left the road and went into the ditch, turning over two or three times before coming to a stop.

By some miracle Earl was able to crawl out. He had a gash across the top of his head from broken glass. The cut in his scalp left the skin pealed back. Pulling himself out and pushing the skin back in place as best he could, he got to his feet and to the nearest house. Up the rather steep hill, through Kingsford's gateway, down to the caretaker's house he walked. When Mrs. Woodard, the caretaker's wife, answered the door she at first did not recognize her neighbor, covered as he was with blood and dirt. She recognized his voice.

"If you will give me a room and a clean shirt," Earl said, "I will get this off." Mrs. Woodard quickly let him in and gave him one of her husband's shirts. Without any help, Earl washed himself off and put on the clean shirt. Someone came from Covewood and took him to Old Forge, where the doctor dressed the wound and put in nine stitches. A few days later, Earl returned to have the stitches removed, but he refused the offer of a local anesthetic.

"I've got my nerve right with me," he said. "I could walk to Thendara" (two miles away). The doctor promptly informed him that he was not walking to Thendara. Earl carried the scar from the accident for a long time. In that difficult and dangerous situation, his presence of mind, his self-reliance and his self-control proved the manner of man that he was. Aside from those accidents and the usual colds of the winter season, our family enjoyed good health. The single exception was our daughter's illness.

Mary Alden's Illness

It was just after Christmas, 1928. There had been a community Christmas tree and a party at Covewood. Our daughter, Mary Alden, then not quite three years old, had a cold but could not bear the thought of missing the party. Her father could see no reason why she should not attend, as the house was warm. I was apprehensive. The hall and stairways were drafty and chilly, but finally, with misgivings, I agreed to her going. She had a good time at the party.

Two or three days passed. On December 28, half-sick with a cold myself, I spent the day in bed. Earl had Mary Alden with him downstairs. That evening when he brought her to bed I took her temperature before tucking her in for the night. I looked at the thermometer. I looked a second time before I could believe my eyes. It registered 104 degrees.

We immediately called Dr. Robert Lindsay in Old Forge. He arrived in a short time. His diagnosis was "pneumonic condition in the lower right lung" — lobar pneumonia. That was before the days of our modern wonder drugs. Recovery from a serious illness was much less certain that it is today. Knowing that Mary Alden would need nursing care, the doctor was able to get for us the services of Miss Lydia Dallaire, a very fine trained nurse who was off duty at the time and at her home in Thendara. She arrived the next day.

From the beginning Mary Alden received the best of care. Even so, Earl was desperately worried. Pneumonia had taken two of his family, and Mary Alden was a very sick child. Earl turned over to his men all work requiring immediate attention, and he took his place at her bedside. He left only long enough to get something to eat at mealtime. He did not go to bed. He caught short naps as he sat there watching, day and night.

For a while Lydia Dallaire was on duty practically around the clock. There was an acute shortage of nurses for private cases at the time, and Lydia had almost reached the point of exhaustion when finally we got a second nurse in relief so that she might have some much-needed rest.

About two weeks after Mary Alden became ill there was a turning point. Both doctor and nurse were watching her chart closely. One day before going off duty Lydia prepared a hypodermic needle containing a solution to be used in a crisis only. She left instructions to call her if needed. She had not been gone long when Earl noted a change in Mary Alden's appearance. He asked the nurse on duty to call Miss Dallaire. Miss W. stepped to the bedside, felt the patient's pulse, and said, "There is no pulse Mr. Covey."

Earl's command was sharp and stern. "Call Miss Dallaire!"

In a matter of seconds Miss Dallaire was at the child's side, administering the hypodermic. Mary Alden rallied. Earl's quick, decisive action undoubtedly saved her life. Miss W. could not remain long on the case and, unable to locate another nurse in the vicinity of Utica, Earl telephoned a physician friend in Albany. In a choked voice he pleaded with Dr. Vander Veer to send the very best nurse he could find. The doctor was able to find us a good practical nurse who remained as long as we needed her.

After the crisis Dr. Lindsay continued to watch our patient's chart even more closely, it seemed, than before. Mary Alden's temperature fluctuated, going first higher then lower. Before her illness reached its critical stage Dr. Lindsay had expressed his willingness to call another physician into consultation if we wished. Anxious to do everything possible to ensure our child's recovery, Earl and I decided we would like a second opinion. So Dr. Lindsay called a lung specialist from Utica to come to Big Moose to make an examination and provide the benefit of his counsel. After examining Mary Alden, Dr. D. said that, while he could not make any definite predictions, he did not think empyema would follow the pneumonia.

For a few days Dr. Lindsay continued to watch the chart, noting the still fluctuating temperature. Finally he decided to make an examination of his own. He inserted a trocar [1.] under the shoulder

---

[1.] A syringe with needle attached.

blade deep into the right lung. His hope was to confirm the cause of congestion as thin fluid, by means of easy withdrawal of the trocar. Instead, the trocar came out with difficulty, filled with pus so thick as to almost clog the needle. The conclusion was that it was empyema.

Robert Lindsay turned and dropped into the nearest chair. He sat for a moment, head bowed, in shock and dismay. Empyema required a rib resection, surgery which, though of a minor nature, called for surgical skill with hospital care. And it had to be done as soon as possible. The doctor explained this all as soon as he could find words to speak. It was the middle of winter. The nearest hospital was seventy miles away in Utica. The afternoon southbound train was due at Big Moose in an hour and a quarter.

The nurses got our patient and themselves ready. I packed a bag for Earl and me while the doctor called for a surgeon, a room at St. Elizabeth's Hospital and an ambulance to meet the train in Utica. Meanwhile, down in the cellar Earl put together a stretcher with sides just high enough to keep our child from falling out and of just the right length to fit into the back of the car. He shaved and changed his clothes.

We left with our housekeeper and one of the other employees in charge. We would be gone for no one knew how long. There had been a recent snowfall, and the car had to make its own track as we left the house and drove out of the yard. On a slight upgrade near the Ainsworth Camp the car almost stalled in the snow — almost, but not quite. We reached the station a few minutes ahead of the train.

Once on the train, we made the remainder of the trip without incident. My father had just arrived from Connecticut to see his granddaughter, and he went with us. The ambulance met the train in Utica to take Mary Alden, accompanied by Earl and Miss Dallaire, to the hospital. Father and I followed in a taxi. A police escort led the way blowing its siren as we proceeded up Genesee Street.

At the hospital we learned that, because she had received her training in Maine, Lydia Dallaire did not have a certificate to practice in a hospital in New York State. She would not be permitted to continue as Mary Alden's nurse. This was a complete surprise. Lydia had nursed our daughter through the most critical days of the illness, and we took it for granted that she would remain on the case. That she could not do so was a keen disappointment to Earl and me as well as to Lydia, herself. While we were able to get a capable nurse in her place, we never ceased to regret that Lydia could not stay on with Mary Alden at the Utica hospital.

Not willing to leave Mary Alden even with a special nurse, Earl decided that he, too, would remain at the hospital. So quietly but so definitely did he make known his intention that the matter was settled before I knew anything about it. There was no serious objection by either doctor or nurse, and it was soon apparent that the child would cooperate with her father more readily than with strangers. Half jokingly Dr. M. called him the "best nurse in the hospital."

For nearly five weeks Earl sat and watched at his daughter's bedside, leaving only at rare intervals. The rib resection was performed the morning after she entered the hospital. Twelve ounces of pus were removed, and a tube was inserted to permit draining to continue from the affected lung.

Earl fit easily into the hospital routine. Only once, and then because he thought it necessary, did he take the situation into his own hands. One evening as he sat watching, Mary Alden seemed unusually restless. Suspecting that something was wrong, Earl asked the nurse to call the doctor. She replied that the doctor was out of town.

"If Dr. M. can't come, we'll have another doctor." Earl meant what he said. Dr. M. arrived within the hour. He found that the tube was not permitting the lung to drain properly, and the draining had stopped. The doctor removed the tube after which the draining continued through the night until another tube was inserted in the morning. Had the draining not resumed the toxic effect of the empyema might have proved fatal. Afterward the doctor told someone that he "put in a bad night" after being called back to the hospital that evening. Again, Earl's decisive action, the second time during her illness, may have saved Mary Alden's life.

It was nearly five weeks before our patient was released from the hospital. Never during that time did Earl show the slightest impatience or complain at being gone from Big Moose so long. But once he knew that the doctor was willing to discharge Mary Alden, he wasted no time in getting her home. From then on I was to be responsible for her care. I was terrified. She had been a very sick child. I was not convinced that she had fully recovered, but she seemed to improve. Earl built an outdoor shelter where she had daytime naps. Later he added a sleeping porch to our bedroom, and she slept there at night.

As it turned out there were grounds for my apprehension. We discovered that when Mary Alden was ready to enter school, she was running a temperature slightly above normal. The doctor advised us that she stay out of school. She was out for two years.

Mary Alden Covey and her mother, Frances Alden Covey, in 1931.

Six years after the first rib resection, she had to have a second one. Again her father went to the hospital and stayed with her for a week while she recuperated from the operation. This time the draining continued from early summer until the following spring.

Throughout that period she saw the surgeon for an examination at regular monthly intervals. Between visits to the doctor Earl changed the bandage on the incision whenever necessary. It was a great relief to me that he was willing to do this. Although it was not a difficult task, I was sure that with his skill he could do it much better than I. The second resection was entirely successful. There was no recurrence of the empyema, and from then on our daughter's health improved rapidly.

Both times Earl had set aside all other work to devote himself to Mary Alden's care. When assured of her recovery, he went back to his job, as busy as ever. Even then he managed to sandwich in among other tasks the building of a little house where she and the other children could play, away from the activity of the main house. Today the Mary Alden Cottage with its little fireplace, and a bath that was added later, provides room for a single guest at Covewood

Lodge.

Even while absorbed in his work Earl was aware of what was going on around him, especially if he thought there was something that needed his attention. One winter before Mary Alden was of school age, I left her in the care of our housekeeper, Mrs. Hamblin, while I was away on a brief visit. During my absence one day she was with her father out of doors. She asked him if she might ride in her cart on the boardwalk between the main house and one of the cottages. He told her not to go. But that was what she wanted to do, and so she took the cart and went for a ride down the walk.

She caught sight of an old cedar tree close to the shore, a favorite haunt in summer. It was great fun to climb out on the leaning tree trunk and look down into the water below. The temptation was apparently irresistible.

Leaving her cart she walked over to the tree and started to climb. The bark was wet and slippery, and she could not maintain her hold. The next thing she knew she was in the lake. Warmly dressed, she did not feel cold. And so she lay there in some two feet of water, enjoying the view. Just then her father appeared. Pulling her out and setting her on her feet, he told her to go to the house, get on some dry clothes and not to tell me.

On my return a few days later I asked Mrs. Hamblin how she had got along in caring for Mary Alden in my absence. I thought she seemed somewhat agitated when she replied but concluded it was just my imagination. For the first few days she allowed Mary Alden to play outside, but later kept her in the house and did not let her out of sight. There was nothing strange about that. Mrs. Hamblin was busy cooking for the men, and she had no time to look for a child wandering around out of doors. I gave the matter no further thought. I have not the slightest doubt that she, too, with Mary Alden, had pledged their secrecy. She never told.

Nor did Mary Alden, during her father's lifetime. Years later, when she told the whole story, I realized that Mrs. Hamblin's agitation was not just in my imagination. She had been agitated, as indeed she had reason to be.

To all outward appearances Earl treated the incident as part of his day's work, returning to the task he had left as though nothing unusual had happened. But — I was not to be told, possibly lest it might have marred the pleasure of my recent visit. Perhaps, too, he did not wish to hear mentioned or even to think of the possible consequence of Mary Alden's ride in her cart down the boardwalk. His watchful care and prompt action saved her from drowning.

Concern for Others

Earl's concern for children was not limited to members of his own family. With the memory of his own child's serious illness in his mind he was deeply concerned a few years later when a little girl at the station fell critically ill with pneumonia. Her condition grew steadily worse. Finally one evening after supper, Earl said, "I'm worried about the little babe. I'm going to see if there is anything I can do." He reached the house as the doctor was leaving.

"There is nothing we can do," he said. As in Mary Alden's case empyema had developed following pneumonia, but it had reached a point where the little one was beyond help. Her death followed shortly afterward. Even though Earl could do no more than express his sympathy and offer his help, his going to the station brought deep comfort to the grief-stricken parents in their time of sorrow.

During Earl's early years at Twitchell a family at the station was destitute because the father spent his earnings on liquor instead of providing for his wife and children. Earl heard of the situation and collected donations for the family from some of the local hotel men. When he approached his father for a donation, Henry Covey asked, "Is that the man who drinks?" Hearing the answer, he refused to contribute. It is doubtful if Henry Covey ever received a more stinging rebuke from anyone than that from his own son when he refused help to those in need through no fault of their own. Earl, the soul of generosity, would share with others as long as he had anything to share.

Like his father, Earl abhorred excessive drinking, but his method of dealing with alcoholics was different from his father's and further evidence of his concern for those afflicted with the habit. In at least four cases Earl reclaimed men from alcoholism. As soon as a man reached the "morning after" stage following a period of drinking,

Earl had a quiet talk with him and persuaded the alcoholic to "take the cure." Then he took the man to a place near Utica where treatment was available, saw him settled there and advanced the necessary money for payment. Drastic and unpleasant though the treatment was, the patient returned after about three weeks, cured of alcoholism. In most cases the cure was permanent.

Earl and My Mother

It was some time before my mother knew Earl well. For a few years she did not even see him. Earl did not accompany me on my early visits to Stafford after marrying nor did she accompany Father when he came to the lake while we were in the Henry Covey Cottage. It was not until we were living in the main house that she visited for the first time.

One September she and Father drove from Connecticut to see us. It was while Mrs. Glenny, a long-time friend and guest of the Coveys at Twitchell, was spending the month with us. She and Mother became acquainted. In some ways the two women were much alike. They were about the same age, and both were outspoken and positive in their opinions. I half expected to see sparks flying between them. But they had one interest in common, their enthusiasm for the game of bridge. Both were good players, and they took their game seriously. They got along very well together.

But they did not spend all their time playing bridge. There were times when they talked together, when Mrs. Glenny told about her summers at Twitchell, about the Coveys, about Earl. Mother listened, and as she saw evidence of his creative skill wherever she looked, she discovered a great deal about her son-in-law that she had not known before.

The day came when my parents were to return to Connecticut. As they prepared to leave, Earl helped to carry the bags to their car. I had gone down the steps and was waiting to see them off. Suddenly Mother, as she stepped out onto the verandah, turned to Earl, and in the tone of one making an important pronouncement, said, "Earl, I am going to kiss you good-bye."

So unexpected was this change in Mother's attitude that for a moment everyone was speechless with surprise. No one could have been more surprised than Earl. Without any attempt on his part to "make a good impression" he had gone about his business, apparently unconcerned with whether Mother liked him or not. By simply being himself he completely won her over.

For the first time, it was apparent that he had been aware of Mother's previous coolness. From then on his attitude toward her was changed as hers was toward him. He was relaxed in her presence, and he laughed and joked with her as he never had before. Even then he never overstepped. From that day on, as long as she lived, Mother was devoted to Earl.

There were several women about Mother's age to whom Earl had been kind and thoughtful and who were very fond of him. Mrs. Clarke was our guest at Big Moose Lake one time when Mrs. Boardman, then managing Twitchell Lake Inn, came to our house on an errand. She was busy that day and planned to go right back.

Earl could see no reason why she should hurry away. He proposed instead that we all go for a ride. He promised Mrs. Boardman that on our return he would take her to Twitchell. The four of us got into our car and drove to Blue Mountain Lake, about thirty-two miles away. The pleasure of deciding to go on the spur of the moment, on that beautiful September day, is still a cherished memory. Someone took a snapshot of Earl and these two "girl friends," one hanging on each of his arms.

Another friend, Mrs. Wheeler, was spending the summer at Twitchell Lake Inn while Earl was helping to run the place during the Second World War. One day when he had an errand in Old Forge he asked her if she would like to go along for the ride. She accepted his invitation and on her return went around proudly boasting to the guests that she had ridden to Old Forge with Mr. Covey. These "girl friends," despite their years, were youthful in spirit, and Earl enjoyed them all.

The Story of the Dogs

Most places in the woods had their household pets. Unless they became too numerous, cats and dogs were like members of the family. At one time there were nine cats at Covewood. As fond as Earl was of animals not even he could make pets of that number. On the other hand, he could never be induced to remove them. To me they were a constant annoyance. When I could no longer endure having them in the kitchen, I would shoo them down the cellar stairs, where they would take refuge behind rows of shelved canned goods. Finally I was able to persuade one of the men to do away with most of them.

With the dogs, however, it was different. At first we had no dogs at Covewood. Later, they were there more by chance than by intention. This is how it happened:

When the Sumner Coveys closed Twitchell Lake Inn and left for the winter, Earl brought Belle, their Newfoundland dog to Covewood. Belle had been with us for a time when she disappeared. No one knew what had become of her. She was a big dog, and I was afraid she had stepped out on the ice near the outlet and broken through.

One January afternoon while Mary Alden and I were out walking, we started toward the Hadden camp, which Earl was building at that time. All of a sudden, from no one knew where, Belle appeared. She walked along with us as far as the Dr. Keese camp, then turning off the trail, she made for the camp. As we watched her, we heard faint sounds coming from Belle's direction. We continued on our way to the Hadden camp where we reported her reappearance and the sounds we heard.

Work on the building stopped immediately, and Earl, with Ross his helper, went right to Keese's. Mary Alden and I watched as the men followed the sounds to the edge of the porch.

Earl crouched down and through a very small opening crawled under the porch. In a few minutes he reappeared, holding in his hat five newborn pups, their eyes not yet open. All this time the mother dog stood by quietly apparently satisfied with the way things were going.

There was a triumphal procession back to Covewood. Earl and the pups led the way followed by Ross. Mary Alden and I brought up the rear. Belle, mother of the pups, came along, too. Arriving at the house Earl made a place for her family in the cellar near the warmth of the furnace. There they remained for about ten days, until their eyes were open. We all watched, some going down several times each day to look at the puppies. After their eyes were open, I suggested to Earl that the pups should have a place with more light, to which he made no immediate reply.

Shortly afterward, without further word to anyone, he decided where the place would be — the family living room. There was no other place for them. They had to be there. He made a pen against one side of the room, with eight-inch planks set edgewise to form the sides. There was plenty of space for the pups as well as for their mother, who came in occasionally to nurse them. We added an old cotton-stuffed quilt for the comfort of the pups and to protect the floor. The quilt had to be washed frequently and the pen kept clean. Earl took care of this himself after the day's work was done.

As they got older the two biggest pups discovered that they could get out of the pen even with a second plank to raise the sides on top of the first. From our room overhead we could hear those two rascals early in the morning as, squealing and barking, they chased each other around the living room. Finally Earl would go and put them back where they belonged. They were great fun during the remainder of the winter, until they were big enough, and the approaching spring months warm enough, to move them outside.

They were handsome pups, black marked with white, and we were able to find homes for all but one, which we kept ourselves. We named her Dinah. She was nearly all black. Dinah was our dog at Covewood and very much a member of the household.

Chapter VI

Covey's Polar Grip Tire

The completion of the main house and five cottages, which made up Covewood, was not the end of Earl's building. But there was an interval during which he divided his time between construction and an absorbing new interest - a natural outgrowth of life in the woods but something that no one else had thought of before. For a few years Earl was both builder and inventor. We have the story of this experience in his own words:

> During the winter of 1928 I had two men working for me. There is quite a hill getting out from my place to the main road. We kept this road plowed out with a team, but nevertheless almost every time we would get stuck, and the men would have to get out and push the Ford up the hill.
> One day I said to them, "Boys, there must be some way that a tire could be made that would give traction and save all this trouble." I began to think about it.
> My first thought was that it must be soft and springy, for I well knew that skis that were hard and stiff were very slippery, while snowshoes that were soft and springy would not slip. My thought then turned to a soft and springy rubber, and I began to experiment with crepe rubber.
> After I had been fussing with crepe rubber for some time, we had occasion to cut and skid quite a number of logs. One day we had a thaw, and our skidding trail became very slippery. The next morning when we went out to work we broke the hook off the chain we were using, and I took the chain down to the shop to weld in a link to replace the hook. In doing so I had to use a bolt for the

Clearing snow from highways and roads was an evolving art. Here in 1928 Earl kept the road from Covewood plowed with a team of horses and a homemade plow. Nevertheless cars frequently had to be pushed up the hill to the main road leading to Inlet.

link. I put it in the forge and heated it, cut off the head and molded the link in with the hook. In doing so I stepped on the bolt head that I had cut off and burned a hole through the sole of my rubber [1] before I was aware of it. The sole, by the way, was crepe rubber.

    I went back to the woods with the chain and worked there till noon. When I came in for dinner my foot was wet, and so I changed my rubbers for a pair with ordinary black rubber soles and went to work. When I got out on the slippery skidding trail, it was so slippery I could hardly stand up. Before that I had not noticed it at all. After working an hour or so, thinking about it all the time, I went down to the house and put the crepe sole rubbers back on. I went back to try them out to see if it was really in the rubber or if it was my imagination. In a short time I was convinced that I had solved a problem.

It was not his imagination. The crepe rubber afforded sure footing on the slippery skidway. The ordinary rubber did not. Clearly the solution lay in the crepe rubber. If it worked on shoes for one's feet,

---

[1] Shoes with leather tops were called rubbers.

Covey's Polar Grip Tire

why not on tires for a car? It had never been tried. No such tires had ever been made.

For several years Mr. J. E. Hale, manager of the Development Department of the Firestone Tire and Rubber Company, had been a guest with his family at Covewood. While he was with us the summer of 1928 Earl had a talk with him and told him that he had an idea for a non-skid tire.

Earl Covey's crepe tire was made as a prototype by the Firestone Company and proved successful in providing traction over ice and snow.

Hale replied, "Don't tell me, but when I get back write to the Company and tell them what you have."

There followed several months of correspondence between Earl and the Company, during which Earl debated whether or not to give them the information. He finally decided to do so. The Development Department proceeded to make him some prototype tires having a tread of pure crepe rubber from a mold specially developed for the purpose. With the coming of snow the next winter, he put them on his station wagon and tried them out.

The new tires proved so satisfactory that Earl made a trip to the factory in Akron, Ohio, to report personally on the success of his tests. The Firestone people were incredulous and thought Earl was exaggerating. But on the strength of what he told them three of their men, including Mr. Hale himself, came to Big Moose to conduct tests of their own. In a letter to a friend, Earl wrote.

> One of the tests we made was to scrape the snow right down to the ice from Rosewood Cottage to my bridge across the outlet. We drew water up the hill in barrels and flooded the road and let it

Three men from the Firestone Tire and Rubber Co. came to Big Moose to see for themselves just how effective the prototype tires were. When they saw what the Covey tire could do they agreed to make enough in a special order to outfit some forty cars. Firestone called it the Polar Grip.

freeze over night. It was like a window light the next morning, just glare ice.

Mr. Roberts [one of the Firestone men] tried ten times with my Chandler [car] to get up the hill with their non-skid tires and chains. When he did reach the top, he came right back and we changed tires. We put mine on without chains and drove to the top the first time without any hesitation whatever.

When the Firestone men saw for themselves what the Covey tires would do, they were convinced that the crepe rubber had better traction than that of ordinary tires. In a telephone conversation from Covewood to the factory Roberts went so far as to say that, with respect to traction, Earl's tires were one hundred per cent better than Firestone's.

Earl received his first tires from the factory in December 1929. Later, enough more were shipped to equip some forty cars in the vicinity. That was an exciting winter. Earl had a wonderful time with his tires. Like a child with a new toy, he would come home after a ride on the ice and snow with an enthusiastic account of the latest triumph over slippery road conditions. Sometimes when he parked

Covey's Polar Grip Tire

The car with the Covey tires was a great hit pushing through the snow on Big Moose Lake in the winter. The tire proved as popular as it was successful, but its wart-like tread would not wear well enough on bare roads to lead to its large scale commercial production.

the car while doing errands in town he would return to find passers-by gazing curiously at the things on the wheels of his car, strange looking with their wart-like tread. He was always glad to answer questions. If no questions were asked he would get into the car and drive away, apparently unconcerned over the interest shown in his tires. Inwardly, he was chuckling with delight.

Earl's invention met with an enthusiastic response from users in the Big Moose area, as well as in places farther away. An Old Forge coal truck with regular tires had been stuck in the snow over a two-week period "at least one-third of the time." Over a subsequent two-week period, equipped with six crepe rubber tires (dual wheels in the rear), it made deliveries where snow in some spots was forty-five inches deep, without once having trouble.

A physician friend in Spencerport, New York, in a letter to Earl, related his experience: "This afternoon I had a call on a side road that had not been cleaned out. The people told me I would have to walk a distance. I asked a friend to go with me, and we took a shovel and started. We did not have any use for the shovel, I drove right up to the house without any trouble. The tires created quite a sensation here."

As soon as he was convinced of the worth of his invention Earl took steps toward obtaining a patent in the United States and in Canada. It was a long-drawn-out process. The Canadian patent came through first, in a little over two years.

It took four and a half years to obtain the United States patent. The U. S. Patent Office first rejected all the claims that were filed. It later accepted them, but only after Earl, accompanied by an attorney, made a trip to Washington for an interview with people in the Patent Office, to convince them of the worth of his claims.

The tire, though it bore the Firestone name, was made only as a special order for Earl. It did not have the Company's unqualified endorsement. As were others in the industry with whom Earl had correspondence, the Company remained skeptical because of the tire's limited wearing quality.

From them all he got the same reaction. The crepe rubber tread would not wear well on bare roads and would therefore be impractical from a commercial standpoint. Earl always suspected that in some cases the manufacturers preferred to concentrate on their own product rather than develop his.

Earl was well aware that the tire needed a toughening agent to make it longer lasting. In his patent he included a claim for such an agent. Had he been able to continue the tire's development he would have given attention to some means of prolonging its life, while at the same time preserving its power of traction. But for this he had neither the time nor the money, and further development would have been costly.

Although the industry, aside from Firestone, showed little interest in Earl's invention, he continued his efforts to reach as many others as possible by means of letters, newspaper advertising and personal contacts. There was a trip to Canada to interview a manufacturer there. Another was a trip to New York to demonstrate his tire on ice-scraping equipment used to clean the skating rink at Madison Square Garden.

One letter Earl wrote in January 1934 was to Lowell Thomas, the adventurer, traveler and icon of radio journalism who had a popular daily newscast in the 1930's for the National Broadcasting Company.

Covey's Polar Grip Tire

Outfitted with his Polar Grip tires Earl Covey once drove up the bobsled run in Lake Placid, the same bobsled run that had been used in the 1932 Winter Olympics.

In the letter Earl describes his experience on the bobsled run at the site of the 1932 Winter Olympics in Lake Placid.

> I drove up with a car equipped with my Polar Grip tires. I went to the bobsled run and asked the man in charge if I might drive up to the top of the hill where the bob run starts.
>
> His answer was, "You can't get up there." I told him that I had a new tire made for snow and ice and that I would like to try and see if I could drive up. He asked if I had chains on. I told him I didn't.
>
> "Then you must have a d----d lot of faith in those tires. Try if you want, but you won't get far," he said. He opened the gate, and I started up.
>
> The engine got hot, and the radiator boiled, but the wheels did not spin, and I went right along. Knowing from your broadcasts that you have been down that bobsled run I thought you might be interested. With Polar Grips on the wheels and Blue Sunoco [gasoline] in the tank, there was nothing to it. I went up that hill like nobody's business.
>
> Very Truly Yours, E.C.

A week later, Lowell Thomas replied,

> I wish I could thank you in person for your letter. I'd sure like to see those tires.
> Cordially, L.T.

Earl remained confident that his Polar Grip met the needs of winter driving as had no other tire before. However, several factors contributed to its failure to catch on. One was the depression of the 1930's, a time when people had little money to spend. Another was the much-improved snow clearing of public highways, which made less urgent the need for non-skid tires. After 1938, Earl spent his winters in Florida, where he was unable to carry on winter business in the North, and finally he gave up the enterprise.

Despite the fact that Earl's invention never reached large-scale production, it is interesting to note the current preference for specialized tires for use in conditions with ice and snow. Winter tires have been developed despite the continuing advancement of highway snow clearing.

A friend of Earl's, formerly engaged in the business of selling cars, said, "Do you realize that until Earl invented his tire no one had ever heard of a winter tire?" It is possible that the Polar Grip [2] stimulated the advancement in tire manufacturing from its beginning on that day when Earl Covey burned a hole in the crepe rubber of his woodsman's shoe.

---

[2] The name Polar Grip was first used by the Firestone Tire & Rubber Co. to designate the Covey crepe rubber tire. Covey's tire never reached the level of mass production, but one of the tires is conspicuously displayed as part of the permanent collection at the Adirondack Museum at Blue Mountain Lake.

Chapter VII

Big Moose Community Chapel

The late 1920's and early 30's were productive years for Earl Covey. It was during that time that he conceived the idea of a crepe rubber non-skid automobile tire. It was then, too, that he designed and directed the building of Big Moose Community Chapel.

Since 1893 there had been religious services at Big Moose Lake. Sometimes they were in a private camp, sometimes at one of the hotels. If a visiting clergyman was present he conducted the service and preached a sermon. Otherwise campers and hotel guests met for a simple song service. For several years there had been Sunday evening "hymn-sings" at Twitchell Lake Inn.

December of 1926 marked the beginning of Protestant services among residents living in the Big Moose area the year round. Until then, only in times of special need was a minister called from the Presbyterian church in Inlet or Old Forge. The first services were in the schoolhouse at the Station, conducted by the Reverend Herbert Baird, minister of the Church of the Lakes at Inlet. Subsequently some of the services were at the Big Moose Lake schoolhouse, to accommodate as many as possible in different parts of the community. In 1927 the Big Moose congregation became affiliated with the Inlet church as the Chapel of the Church of the Lakes.

During the summer, always a busy time for the local people, the services, attended mostly by campers and hotel guests, centered at Big Moose Lake. As they had in the past, the hotels in turn provided the place of meeting, usually the recreation room of the boathouse.

A particularly interesting feature of the Chapel's summer program was the Sunday School, which met in the boathouse of Dr. Albert Vander Veer Sr. Each Sunday morning Romaine Kinnie's largest launch made the rounds of camps on the lake to take children to Sunday School at the Vander Veer camp. At the end of the hour the boat returned to take them home again. So popular was the Sunday School, perhaps the boat ride had something to do with it, that the Chapel engaged a special worker, who with volunteers directed the program of the Sunday School.

Plans for a Church Building

Meanwhile people at Big Moose were beginning to think of a place more permanent and better suited to public worship than the schoolhouse or a boathouse, useful though both had been as temporary expedients.

As a result, at the end of the summer season, on September 17, 1928, the congregation voted to erect a church building. Two committees were formed to make plans and proceed with construction. Dr. Albert Vander Veer Sr., was chairman of the finance committee. Earl Covey headed the building committee. Both went to work immediately, the former to secure funds, the latter to find a suitable location.

The finance committee's appeals for money brought an immediate response. Checks and pledges began to come in, and several local residents pledged labor and material.

The building committee began to investigate every available site both at the Station and Big Moose Lake. Some months prior to this Earl, saying little about it to anyone, purchased land at the Station to hold for the Chapel should no other site be found.

After a thorough canvass of the area and considerable debate, the committee recommended and the congregation agreed to purchase a lot from Nelson Dunn Sr. between his home and that of Dr. Charles Walker. The price was $2,000. The beauty of the spot, combined with its accessibility from the lake and the road, made the site ideal.

In order to obtain an estimate of its cost the finance committee drew up specifications for the new building and then asked Earl if he thought he could build according to those specifications. Without spending time to study the figures, Earl took a quick glance at the sheet handed to him and then, to the amusement of the finance committee member, asked, "How big do you want it?"

The dimensions were agreed upon. The main part of the building, to be used for regular worship services, would be seventy feet long and thirty-two feet wide. A wing, for the Sunday School and other groups, would be thirty-two feet long and twenty-two feet wide.

Earl apparently satisfied the finance committee that he could build according to their specifications. They instructed him to proceed without delay. With his men and team of horses he broke ground, and by the end of October he was ready to start on the building itself.

Following the September meeting, at which the congregation voted to erect a church building, the finance committee submitted an estimate of $15,000 on a wooden frame building, including furnishings and equipment. Earl's estimate, for a stone building, was $18,000. The members of the finance committee, much as they would have liked stone, did not think they could raise $18,000.

Earl recalled the substantial Roman Catholic churches of brick or stone he had seen on his trips to Canada, many of them out in the country or in small communities. In striking contrast the Protestant churches were of wood construction, sometimes in run-down condition. This made an impression on Earl. He occasionally mentioned those churches when recalling his trips, before a Protestant church at Big Moose was ever thought of.

Late in October Earl sent a letter to Dr. Percy Wightman, a member of the finance committee. The following, in part, is what he wrote:

> Your letter of yesterday just received and I went over it very carefully. If your committee thinks that $18,000 is beyond them, then perhaps we had better figure on a wood building. I seem to be the only one sticking out for a stone building, and I don't want the people to think that I am trying to get them to do anything that is out

of reason.

The estimate for a wood building was made by other members of the committee. I did not figure on the wood building at all myself. I doubt if we could build it of stone and hire it done, for less than $25,000. But on the other, hand, if we do it ourselves and are willing to give our time for less than half what we would have to pay other men for the same work, besides giving a good liberal amount outright, we can build it for the $18,000 including the lot and furnishings. But if it is a case of cutting that amount [by] $2,000, then it is beyond me.

I have the digging pretty well along and started the cellar wall on one side today, and I ought to know definitely just what is going to be built at once. It is getting late and we will have snow in a short time, and if I put the job through I will have to do it when I can without tying up my own place entirely.

The letter continued:

There will also have to be some arrangement made so that bills can be paid promptly at this end. You see the situation is this: I am the only one giving time now. Everyone wants to hunt, and so I have to hire men to get anything done, and of course men have to be paid. When I ordered a car of cement three weeks ago, I bought it for cash in order to get the very best price, which was about one dollar per barrel less than any cement that has come to the lake this summer. Some arrangement should be made to take care of such bills.

In conclusion he wrote, "Trusting everything will come out O K which I am sure it will ... with best wishes ...

It was apparent that the matter of material to be used could not very well be settled by writing letters back and forth. Consequently Dr. Wightman, the busy pastor of University Heights Presbyterian Church in New York City, decided to make a trip to Big Moose so that he might talk with Earl personally. One day not long afterward he arrived on the afternoon train to spend the night at Covewood. He brought with him an estimate on a wooden building, which Dr. Vander Veer had obtained from an Albany architect. It is more than possible that he had been authorized to arrive at a decision with Earl while at Big Moose as to the kind of building the new church was to be, wooden or stone.

That evening after supper the two men sat down with the estimate for a wooden building. They discussed it from every angle, each listening carefully to what the other had to say. The evening passed. It was getting late. Bedtime came. There was no decision.

After breakfast the next morning there was more discussion. It was nearing train time, and Dr. Wightman had to go. There was still no decision. The men continued talking as Dr. Wightman put on his coat and picked up his hat. Earl and I accompanied him to the door. As he bade our guest good-bye Earl said, "If the building is of wood I will contribute money. If it is of stone I will supervise the work and it won't cost much more."

With his hand on the doorknob, Dr. Wightman turned to Earl and smiled. "All right," he said. "Make it of stone." And with that he walked out the door to the car that was waiting to take him to the station.

That brief overnight visit accomplished what had not been possible through weeks of the finance committee's deliberations. It gave them assurance of Earl's full cooperation and that he would see the job through. It also assured them that the cost of the stone, while more than that of wood, would not be excessive.

At no time in their conversations at Big Moose did Earl bring undue pressure on Dr. Wightman in favor of stone. It was rather a gradual, patient building up of his case for its use. Dr. Vander Veer's committee wanted stone from the beginning. From their point of view it was merely a question of cost, a very important consideration because it was to be their task to raise the money. During Dr. Wightman's visit to Big Moose, Earl was able to convince him, and through him the other members of the committee, that the cost would not be too great. In the final analysis it was because of their confidence in Earl that the finance committee decided to proceed with stone rather than wood.

With the decision made to use stone the next task was to get it. There was an open vein of granite in the quarry at Dart's Mountain, and it was from there that Earl got the stone. As soon as he could

By October 1928 site preparation was underway even while discussion continued as to the merits and costs of constructing the chapel with wood or with stone. After little more than a beginning, snow stopped work at Christmas time, but Big Moose was going to have a chapel.

move his air compressor to the spot he began drilling and blasting the rock into slabs six and eight feet in length. Cut into smaller pieces, these were loaded on a stoneboat and hauled by team down to the highway over a short but rough and narrow tote road. From there they were hauled to the building site, a distance of two and a half miles. With winter approaching there was time for little more than a beginning before the snow became so deep as to make work at the quarry impossible, and at Christmas time work was discontinued until spring. This was the winter of our daughter's long illness when Earl remained for weeks at her bedside. He was also distracted by his invention of a crepe rubber non-skid tire. The early part of 1929 was a particularly busy time for him.

With the coming of spring work at the quarry resumed. Earl made a practice of employing local men whenever possible. For specialized work like plumbing and masonry he found it necessary to

Work resumed in the spring of 1929 as soon as Covey and his men could get back into Dart's quarry. Slabs were cut six and eight feet in length. Then cut into smaller pieces they were hauled by horse teams to the building site, two and half miles away.

bring in outside help. Stonework for the Chapel was a very special job, and he was fortunate in securing the services of Louis Panunzio, a skilled stonecutter from Malone, New York. Louis brought his wife and young son with him, and the family was given the use of the old Rose Cottage rent free with no additional charge to the Chapel.

At times the cutting and laying of the stone seemed endless. Day after day the two men chiseled and pounded stone until their fingers, even with protecting gloves, were raw to the point of bleeding. But they kept on, and gradually, as the days lengthened into weeks, the walls rose, stone by stone. During the early stage of building, Dr. Wightman, having seen somewhere a church with a fireplace, asked Earl, "Are you going to build a fireplace in the Chapel?" Until then no one had thought of a fireplace. But following the suggestion Earl built a fireplace of Malone sandstone

At times the cutting and setting stone seemed endless. Covey and Louis Panunzio, a skilled stone cutter from Malone, New York, pushed on, and gradually as the days lengthened through the summer, the walls appeared row by row.

at the rear of the sanctuary.

J. Hillis Miller, First Summer Minister

Because the pastor of the Church of the Lakes had the church and congregation in Inlet as his chief responsibility, members of the Chapel decided to look for someone who could give full time to the work at Big Moose. They found Joseph Hillis Miller, who was doing graduate work at Columbia University and serving as assistant to Dr. Harry Emerson Fosdick, pastor at the time of Riverside Church in New York City.

After some correspondence, followed by his visit to Big Moose for a first-hand view of the situation, Hillis accepted the position of summer minister. His decision was doubly fortunate for the Chapel in that it provided not only a minister but also his wife, Nell Miller,

With the arrival of J. Hillis Miller as a summer pastor for the congregation and increased contributions in the building fund, work on the chapel took on new meaning for Covey and his workers. The walls were completed and a roof in place before snow fell in December 1929.

as a director of the summer Sunday School program. In June 1929, the Millers with their small son, Hillis Jr., arrived for their first summer at Big Moose.

The expanded program of the Chapel made the summer of 1929 a busy and interesting one for the entire community. The arrival of the Millers provided new impetus to the work. Under Mrs. Miller's capable direction the young people met for Sunday School each Sunday morning, transported in Kinne's big boat to and from the Vander Veer boathouse.

Hillis, through the Sunday services and through his daily contacts, availed himself of every opportunity to meet as many people as possible, to acquaint them with the work of the Chapel and to interest them in the new building. Keen, forceful and dynamic, his was a compelling personality with a strong appeal to students and young people, of whom there were many attending the services. One would often hear the give-and-take about the sermon between the young preacher and a member of the congregation as people were leaving the Sunday service. Now and then someone would go back and continue the discussion after the others were gone.

All of this, the message and the personality of the summer minister and the prospect of a new church building, had its impact on life at the lake and was reflected in a new enthusiasm, evidenced in the increased contributions to the Chapel building fund.

Meanwhile the women, calling themselves the Willing Workers, organized for the purpose of raising money. They held a most successful bazaar in the Glenmore boathouse, the first of many to be held for the benefit of the Chapel.

The first Guides Supper was that summer of 1929, when the Chapel walls were just high enough to show window openings on each side. The supper was cooked outdoors and served at tables close to the lake. Some of the meat, broiled over a fire built on the fireplace foundation of the unfinished building, was carried down the hill and served on tables below. The occasion engaged the time and energies of many in the community.

It was a good summer. It was so successful, in fact, with the Millers there that everyone wanted them back the next year. There was a challenge in the situation, and Hillis liked anything that challenged. The Millers agreed to return.

Dr. Vander Veer's Death

Through the fall Dr. Vander Veer kept in touch with work on the Chapel, making visits to the building whenever he was at the lake. Now that he had retired from medical practice this new undertaking had become his chief interest, and to it he gave as generously of his time and means as he had to the religious work at the lake in the past. He and Earl, as chairmen of their respective committees, worked closely together.

The Old Doctor, as he was affectionately called, was no stranger to the Coveys, having known them over the years to the second and third generation. That, which they were doing together, strengthened the bond between them. Earl kept the Doctor informed by frequent letters and by pictures taken from time to time to show the progress made. He never seemed to have the slightest doubt that the necessary funds would be forthcoming. On one occasion when the building account was low, the Doctor expressed anxious concern in a letter to Earl. To which Earl replied, "Don't worry about the money, everything will come out all right."

The confidence of the younger man brought comfort and assurance to the older. The relationship between them was akin to that of father and son. Someone took a picture of the two men standing at the front doorway of the Chapel, the partly finished walls forming the background.

With the coming of colder weather the Doctor returned to his home in Albany, where he continued for a time to keep in touch with the work at Big Moose. Several weeks followed when no letters came from him. A member of the family wrote that his strength was failing.

Dr. Vander Veer did not live to see the building finished. His death a short time later, in December 1929, made it necessary for others to carry on in his place. But to the very end his thoughts were of this new undertaking at the lake. One of his last requests was that a picture of the Chapel be buried with him. The picture chosen was that of the Doctor and Earl as they stood together in the Chapel doorway.

When the Old Doctor saw the Chapel for the last time, the walls were still under construction. There had to be a roof on the building before winter if it was to be ready for use the following summer. As had happened many times in the past, Earl had to make every minute count. Once again he won the race against time. The walls were completed, and the roof was on before snow fell.

The inside finishing began. Other than the men working with him, very few knew Earl's plan for the interior. Apparently everyone was willing to leave this for him to decide, and if he ever discussed it with others it was done verbally and informally, because Chapel records make no mention of the interior finish.

Soon birch paneling appeared, set off by strips of darker cherry in pleasing contrast. Logs of peeled spruce swept overhead in beams, joists and rafters. Only then did we know how the inside of the Chapel was going to look. Earl himself said little, in modesty perhaps, because much of the material was a gift from him. Perhaps, too, by "keeping quiet" until all was done he could bring even to this serious and difficult task that element of surprise that always delighted him.

The Chapel Fire (1930)

By the start of the summer of 1930 the Millers had returned and the Chapel was nearing completion. Though still unfinished, it was in shape to use. The first service in the new building was planned for Sunday, July 20. There were no pews and no organ. We purchased folding chairs, and someone loaned a piano.

On Saturday workers, both men and women, gave the paneling its final rubbing with linseed oil, swept the floors, gathered up oily rags to be burned and put the chairs in place. By seven thirty that evening everything was ready for the service the next day. By nine o'clock, after a choir practice, everyone had gone home.

It was about half past ten. Earl and I had gone upstairs for the night when the telephone rang. A voice called, "The Chapel is on fire!"

Just what happened immediately afterward will forever remain a blank in my mind. Somehow the Millers, next door, were notified. In their car the four of us reached the Chapel in a matter of minutes.

A crowd, already gathered, stood dumb, helpless, horror stricken. The whole interior was ablaze. Fire engines from Inlet and Old Forge had been called to a small fire at the Station shortly before, and they were on the scene almost immediately. But there was no pump to which the hose could be attached, no facilities for bringing water from the lake. In less than two hours the work of months was destroyed. The spruce beams, the birch paneling that had been peeled and rubbed by hand, the plate glass windows. All were gone.

So complete was the destruction that it was impossible to discover how the fire started. There was much discussion, much conjecture. That it might have been incendiary was ruled out. There had been no ill feeling in the community concerning the Chapel nor had there been any toward those engaged in its work. There was no one, so far as we knew, who was mentally deranged and might have committed such an act. It was suggested that some passer-by, stepping inside, might have carelessly dropped a lighted cigarette or that spontaneous combustion from an oil-soaked rag, overlooked in cleaning up might have been the cause. Nothing was left by way of evidence to furnish proof of either. To this day the origin of the Chapel fire is a mystery unsolved.

What Earl lived through that awful night would have crushed anyone less stouthearted. He had to stand helpless while flaming disaster, swift and terrible, swept away that which had become part of his life. Someone saw him alone, away from the crowd, sobbing, grief-stricken. Next to the loss of a member of his family this was the nearest to tragedy he had ever known.

As the flames subsided and there was nothing more that could be done at the Chapel that night, people gradually left the scene, dazed, wondering what could be done. Nothing was left of the building except the bare outside walls. The Millers joined us for a while in our living room on our return to Covewood. Still overcome with shock and grief, Earl could not talk. Our friends, giving what comfort and assurance they could, finally said good night and went on to their cottage. But later, before the fire had time to burn itself out, Earl exclaimed in a voice choked and broken, "We will do it!"

The next morning many of us returned to the Chapel to see by daylight the extent of the damage and to decide if possible, what to do next. One of our number, Mrs. Nancy Ellsworth, stood looking at what remained of the Chapel. Then she sobbed, "To think this had to happen after all Mr. Covey's hard work!" Indeed, the loss to Earl was staggering.

But the loss was not Earl's alone. The loss was shared by all who, like Nancy Ellsworth, had worked so hard and so faithfully to make the building possible. Many had given as they were able of their time, talent and material, and many had given money. They included year round residents at the Station, Big Moose and Twitchell Lakes, and summer campers and guests throughout the area. Suddenly the Chapel was gone, and no one could see the way ahead.

Restoration and Dedication

Meanwhile, however, Hillis Miller, wasted no time in arranging a service for that afternoon in the boathouse of Lakeview Lodge. He asked the Reverend Frank Reed, then pastor of Niccolls Memorial

Church in Old Forge, to lead the congregation in prayer. It was fitting that, as minister in charge of our winter services, Mr. Reed should be called on at this crucial time in the life of the Chapel. Perhaps too, Hillis dared not try to take that part of the service himself. The night before, with all that had happened, was still too close.

Prayer is the only part of the service I remember. In it Frank Reed expressed our sorrow, our need of strength and courage for the task ahead and our hope that somehow that which had been taken from us might be restored.

Before the day was over sufficient funds had been pledged to restore the loss. Typical of the spirit of the people at Big Moose are the following excerpts from a letter to Earl written by Dan Ainsworth, a long-time friend and fellow Chapel worker:

> Dear Friend:
> I was down at the Chapel all yesterday afternoon keeping the crowd from coming in too fast for fear someone might be injured.
> It sure is a terrible blow to us all but much more to you after all the months you have worked. ... You have my sympathy. Now, Earl, what is to be done first?
> I am called away for two days on a camping trip. Will see you as soon as I return.

The first thing to be done was to ascertain the extent to which the outside walls had suffered damage. It was found that the tower and front wall down to the entrance required rebuilding, and the granite memorial cross over the doorway would have to be replaced. Walls of the sides and back had come through unharmed.

On Monday morning Earl and his men went back to clear away the blackened ruins, all that was left of the Chapel's interior. The job was hard enough, at best. Had it not been for the generosity, the sympathy and moral support of the entire community the task would have been heartbreaking. For Earl it was this that sustained him and gave courage for the difficult days immediately following the fire.

At no time was there any faltering or turning back. With removal of the debris the rebuilding began under Earl's direction. The women meanwhile put on their second annual bazaar in the boathouse of the old Glenmore Hotel. On the same day the men cooked their second outdoor supper at the Chapel. Both bazaar and supper brought people together in a renewed spirit of enthusiastic cooperation. Both events provided substantial contributions to the Restoration Fund. Another factor that contributed to community interest in the work of the Chapel was Hillis Miller's decision to hold not one service on Sunday but two. One was in a boathouse at one end of the lake in the morning and the second at the other end in the afternoon. There was good attendance at both services.

By the end of the summer the restoration of the Chapel, which was to take another year to complete, was well under way. A new tower, front wall and memorial cross replaced those that had been destroyed in the fire. A new roof was put on the building, and new glass was put in the windows, thus again enclosing the building so that work could proceed during the winter. The fireplace was rebuilt.

Beams and rafters of spruce, peeled and polished, were again fit in place. These new pieces were larger and better proportioned than those in the first structure. One beam, fifty-six feet long, was brought down from Billy's Bald Spot by Earl's big horses over a hillside so steep that they had to make the descent on their haunches to keep the long "stick" from moving too rapidly. The inside walls were again of birch with cherry for battens and wainscoting. As before, the panels in the gable ends lifted one's admiring view upward as the eye followed their reach to the rafters overhead.

Finally, early in the summer of 1931, the building, completely restored, was once again ready for use. On the morning of that June Sunday when the first service was to be held, some of us, to whom the 1930 fire was still an all-too-vivid memory, had to reassure ourselves that the Chapel had come through the night safely and was there. At last we had what we had hoped for, and worked for, so long — a suitable place where all who wished might meet and worship together.

The dedication took place in August. On the preceding afternoon the Chapel was a busy place. Some of the women were sweeping up and putting things in order while others were arranging flowers and

The Big Moose Community Chapel captured the hearts and spirits of the community and attracted gifts in the form of cash as well as furnishings. The pews were given in memory of Mr. and Mrs. Clarence Kelsey and the organ in memory of Dr. Albert Vander Veer Sr.

ferns. There were flowers at the front of the room, flowers banking the fireplace at the back, flowers at the windows, flowers in the vestibule. There were flowers everywhere.

In the midst of it all the editor of the local paper was seeking to obtain information from anyone who would stop long enough to answer his questions. By buttonholing one after another he managed to get material for his article. Everywhere there was excitement and anticipation. It was like getting ready for a wedding.

On Sunday, August 2, 1931, the Chapel was dedicated at a morning and an afternoon service. The preacher for the morning service was Dr. James Moffatt, noted Biblical scholar and translator. In the afternoon a friend of Hillis Miller, Rabbi Louis D. Newman of New York City, delivered the address. Mr. Miller and the Chapels' past and present winter ministers took part. The day of dedication was one of gladness and thanksgiving for the people of Big Moose. Later that summer the congregation was incorporated under the name of Big Moose Community Chapel.

The Big Moose Community Chapel literally rose a second time from the ashes of the fire, which destroyed the original building on July 19, 1930, the night before its dedication. The building was gone, but by August the next year this replacement opened its doors to the community.

Memorial Gifts: Pews and Organ

By any measure the Chapel was beautiful. One of the most striking features was its clear glass windows allowing views of the surrounding trees, lake and mountains, unblocked as they might have been by stained glass.

However, no account of the Chapel would be complete without mention of the memorials given, many as cash contributions to the building fund and others in the form of furnishings. Among the latter were the pews in memory of Mr. and Mrs. Clarence Kelsey, from their sons, and the organ, a memorial to Dr. Albert Vander Veer Sr., from his family. These gifts by their very nature were part of the building, and the donors looked to Earl to make the selection and to oversee the installation.

For the pews Earl sought the advice and assistance of Mr. Albert Ayer. The first thing the two men did was to visit Riverside Church in New York to study the pews there. With data they obtained, including two full-length sketches of a pew end, they returned to

Big Moose and went to work preparing specifications for pews for the Chapel at Big Moose. Completed plans were sent to a construction firm in Utica, where the parts were built and shipped to Big Moose for assembly and installation. Many have attended the Chapel services in recent years, but few know the care and planning that went into the building of the pews, how the details of height, seat angle, end design and cushion color were all combined to produce the result of satisfying comfort and beauty.

The Vander Veers in considering their gift at first had a reed organ in mind. Earl had some conversation with members of the family, and there was correspondence by mail. He knew about how much they thought they could put into their memorial. Thinking in terms of a pipe organ, Earl began to look into the possibility of such an instrument for the Chapel.

In the course of his investigation he became acquainted with C. E. Morey, a pipe-organ builder in Utica who had installed several of his instruments in that area. Earl listened to a Morey organ at the Utica plant, as did several friends at his request. All were impressed by the quality of its tone.

But the cost of a pipe organ was more than the Vander Veers had expected to pay. There were conversations between Earl and Mr. Morey. Then the latter made a trip to Albany, where there was still another conversation, this time between Morey and the Vander Veers. Morey quoted them his lowest possible price on an instrument, which he considered suitable for the setting. Friends contributed to the cost, and the necessary amount was finally raised.

What the Chapel Meant to Earl

With the completion of Big Moose Chapel, Earl turned his attention to other matters, among them the annual Guides Supper. His enthusiasm led to cooperation among both summer and year-round residents, and the supper was a great success. For years, ordering the food, putting up the tables and cooking the steak and chicken were all under his supervision. No one worked harder, or enjoyed the Guides Supper more, than Earl himself.

As the first summer minister, Hillis Miller was with the Chapel during its period of building. When cutting and laying the stone seemed an endless task, Hillis was there to encourage and give moral support. His faculty for winning friends for the Chapel resulted in many contributions to the building fund and was a constant surprise and delight to those associated with him. He keenly enjoyed those contacts. There would be an unmistakable twinkle in his eye as he reported, almost casually, that So-and-So was making a gift to the Chapel. The restoration following the fire was due in no small measure to the wholehearted manner in which he embraced the undertaking and saw it through.

During those early years Hillis was very important to the Chapel. He was wonderfully important to Earl as well. It would have been difficult to find two men more unlike with respect to age, background and education than Earl Covey and Hillis Miller. Earl, in his middle fifties, was born and reared in a remote area of upstate New York where the opportunities for education were limited. He had spent most of his life in a small Adirondack community, and there he did most of his work. Hillis, a Virginian by birth and much younger, already had an impressive background of study, preaching and teaching and was on his way to a brilliant career in the field of higher education.

Yet in their common devotion to the Chapel the differences between them mattered little. With an incredible capacity for work, unhampered by self-seeking or conflicting motives, they faced their task together with faith and courage, which permitted no obstacle to stand in their way. It was this spirit that first brought the Chapel into being and later, after a disastrous fire, caused it to rise again from the ashes, restored. The association between Earl and Hillis as they worked to achieve their goal, the high regard of each for the other, united them in a bond of friendship, which lasted as long as they lived.

The Chapel added a new dimension to Earl's life. In the inspiration of its services of worship, in the friendships he formed there, in the love and honor accorded him by friends and strangers alike, he found a renewal of his own spirit, which repaid him a thousand fold for the toil and sacrifice the Chapel had cost him. Before he could even step into the aisle at the close of a Sunday service people pressed forward to greet him and clasp his hand.

Sunday became a day set apart. Throughout the afternoon hours he relived the service of the morning, recalled parts of the sermon, the goodly number in attendance, the friends he had met. All of this the Chapel meant to Earl and more, much more than any words he could express. He carried that hour of worship into his daily living as he went about his work in the week that followed. The Chapel had become part of him.

Mr. Colpitts' Gift

While the Chapel was Earl's crowning achievement it was by no means the end of his building. Some of his finest work was done later, after the Chapel, when he built several camps on Big Moose Lake, one at Twitchell and another on Fourth Lake.

One of those camps at Big Moose Lake, built for Mr. Walter Colpitts, was in the nature of an experiment, different from anything Earl had done before. Mr. Colpitts wanted to try using Cemestos wallboard, a product of the Celotex Company, for an entire building including the outside walls. Fern Spring Camp in South Bay, which he had purchased, was the scene of his experiment. Buildings on the property were removed, and work began on the new one.

Cemestos, like other kinds of wallboard, was made in sheets eight feet long and four feet wide. The difference was in its greater thickness. Cemestos came two inches thick. The only other materials in the walls of the camp were two-by-fours, which joined the sheets of Cemestos. To the astonished relief of the next-door neighbor who had expected to hear blows of a hammer all day long, there was no pounding to be heard while the building was under construction. There were no nails to pound. The two-by-fours were secured to the Cemestos by six-inch screws.

The new camp was an experiment literally from the ground up. Cemestos, set down to the ground, served as a wall around the outside of the building as well as forming its sides. Mr. Colpitts even tried using Cemestos for the roof, but this did not prove satisfactory and was replaced by steel roofing. Some years later the part next to the ground was cut away to permit freer ventilation under the house. Aside from these changes, and some interior repairs, the camp stands as Mr. Colpitts built it in the early 1940's, the brown exterior shading into the trees, which partly surround it. It is one of a group of cottages on the South Bay shore of Big Moose Lake.

To Earl, always intrigued with the new and the different, the rebuilding of Fern Spring Camp was an absorbing interest. And he valued his contact with Mr. Colpitts. When the building, completed, was ready for its owner, Earl said, and there was a catch in his voice as he spoke, "I think he will like it."

Mr. Colpitts did like it. He had a place of his own on the lake, and he liked Fern Spring Camp well enough to regard it as a suitable gift to the Chapel, to be used as a manse for the summer minister. Walter Colpitts, moreover, enjoyed his contact with Earl. Although he had a wide acquaintanceship in the fields of business, banking and education, he once told someone that Earl Covey was one of the finest men he ever knew.

But all of this about Fern Spring Camp, the summer manse of Big Moose Chapel, is ahead of my story. To go back:

The completion of the Chapel in 1931 was followed by several years of building. But approaching sixty years of age, Earl was finding work more difficult than that in the past. The chief reason was his arthritis, which was becoming increasingly painful. By the end of 1937 he had given up most of his building. We had not recovered from the Depression, and the burden of work and the financial responsibility involved in the operation of Covewood were becoming more than he felt able to carry. Earl talked of selling the property.

Earl had tried various so-called remedies for arthritis. He spent several weeks at a sanitarium, where he lost much weight and showed little improvement. One of the doctors there suggested that he try Florida. In a desperate hope of obtaining relief he decided to act on the doctor's advice and see what a month in the Florida sunshine would do. On a day late in March we loaded our bags into the car and started south. Clearwater, on Florida's Gulf coast, was our objective.

Chapter VIII

The Later Years

First Trip to Florida

We found an apartment at Clearwater Beach overlooking the Gulf of Mexico, and as soon as we were settled Earl found a spot where he could sit in the sun. Until then he had never seriously thought of going to Florida. An extended stay seemed impossible, and a short trip, only to return to the cold and snow of an Adirondack winter, did not appeal to him at all.

But there he was, sitting in the sunshine and taking an occasional dip in the salt water. In the late afternoon, when it became too cool to be outdoors, he sat by the living room window where he could look out across the waters of the Gulf to the glory of a Florida sunset, a brief but gorgeous pageant of ever-changing color.

Earl's month in Florida may have brought him some relief from arthritis. It certainly afforded him a change of scene, a new experience and something different to think about. We said little about returning another year. I already had, as they say, "Florida sand in my shoes," although I tried not to appear too enthusiastic because the decision on this matter should be Earl's to make not mine. But he, too, had Florida sand in his shoes. Before we left the Sunshine State that month we purchased a lot near Clearwater with the intention of building a house on it.

Lease of Covewood

That year, 1938, was a time of change for Earl Covey. He made his first trip to Florida, after which, on our return, another change was to occur. We had begun to make plans for the coming season at Covewood when we received word from the Lake George realtor with whom we had listed the place for sale. A Mr. Walter Reid was looking for an Adirondack resort to lease. Did we care to talk with him?

Earl was not in favor of a lease. He knew that a lessee sometimes "milked" property — used it for his own benefit without attempting to put back what had been taken out in the way of damage or abuse. Earl did not want any property of his treated that way. But he told the realtor he would talk with Mr. Reid, if the latter wished to come to Big Moose to see him.

A day or so later Walter Reid came to Covewood for an interview. He stated his proposition, which we spent an evening discussing from every angle. Earl voiced his objection to a lease, and Reid said he understood Earl's point of view. But the former was not in a position to buy. He assured Earl, however, that any property he leased would not be "milked."

It was not possible for either one to reach a decision that evening. When Mr. Reid left that night they agreed that he would telephone the next day to let us know whether he had decided to lease the property, provided he had Earl's consent.

Before the call in the morning Earl was to decide whether, under an arrangement not altogether satisfactory to him, he would turn over the operation of Covewood to a stranger, someone he had never seen before. This was home for him and his family. Into it he had put some of his finest work. It would mean pulling up stakes, moving out and finding another place to live at a time when he was almost completely unable to work.

On the other hand, a lease now might lead to a sale later, and Earl had definitely decided to sell. His impaired health and the fact that he was no longer young made it urgently necessary that he ease the load that he had carried for so long. There had to be a change sooner or later. Perhaps this was the time.

In the summer following the first trip to Florida, Frances, Earl and Mary Alden were back in Big Moose with their Newfoundland, Dinah. The weather had been helpful for Earl, and as Frances would say, they had sand in their shoes. However, the transition from state to state and school to school was less than ideal for Mary Alden. Four years later she would enroll at the Northfield School for Girls in Massachusetts.

Knowing all this, weighing one consideration against another, Earl had to make his decision overnight. Walter Reid had less than two months in which to hire workers and get Covewood ready for the summer business. He had to make up his own mind and know what Earl wanted to do, without further delay.

For the Coveys, the decision had to be Earl's. Knowing nothing about such things, I was of little help. In the evening's discussion Mr. Reid's answers to my questions were slanted, naturally, in favor of a lease until I began leaning toward that point of view myself. But I was by no means convinced. Earl had what he considered good and sufficient reasons for not wanting a lease, and I was willing to abide by his judgment. Thus the matter stood when we went to bed.

Morning came, and Earl, after a wakeful night, was half-asleep when the telephone rang. Before going downstairs I stepped to his bedside to ask what answer he wanted me to make should the call be from Reid.

"I wonder if we should do it?" were his first words, in the faint tones of one barely awake. He seemed still so uncertain, so troubled, that I said, "If you don't want to, we can call the whole thing off."

"Well," he said, "we'd better be sports and go through with it."

That was Earl's answer. With that I went downstairs to the telephone. The call was from Walter Reid. He would like to lease Covewood, if that was agreeable to us. I replied by letting him know Earl's decision. A few days later the three of us met at the realtor's office to sign the necessary papers and settle other details in connection with the transaction. Earl signed his name, but he did so with a heavy heart.

Our New Home

In order to give Mr. Reid time to get Covewood ready for the summer, we began preparations for moving out at once. The obvious plan, it seemed to me, was to rent a house until we had one of our own.

Earl had a different idea. Part of the estate he had inherited from his father was a lot along the outlet on the shore across from Covewood. He decided to start building a house there right away, and he immediately set his men to work clearing the ground.

While this was going on he remarked once or twice that there should be some sort of a plan for the house. In the rush and excitement of getting ready to move, I had not even thought of such a plan. Earl knew what we should have, and he knew better than I did what we could have in the short time available for building. Having nothing just then to suggest, I went on with what I was doing without making a reply. Finally one evening he said again, "We've got to decide what we want. We're starting the building tomorrow."

I realized that I was expected to offer some suggestion. I had to think quickly — the work was starting tomorrow. I proposed something that had been in the back of my mind, the one and only feature I could think of. I wanted a "den," a separate room large enough for Earl's desk, a sewing machine and a typewriter. It would be apart from the living room, freeing the latter from workroom clutter and making easier the task of keeping it in order. On this suggestion Earl offered no comment. I dared not ask if he approved, because if he had not, I could not have thought of an alternative to save my life. He seemed willing to accept the idea. At least he raised no objection. Work began the next day.

Still too crippled to work himself, Earl could only supervise the building and keep the men supplied with material. But thanks to their speed and efficiency, in less than four weeks the house was ready. We moved in with our belongings, at least with most of them. Some things, overlooked in packing, were left behind. The last of the Covey possessions to be moved were some Twitchell Inn and Camp Crag records that Earl had stored away years before. I had never seen them. More than twenty years after we left they were discovered while Covewood's owner was cleaning out the attic.

Despite the haste, the work of building the house was well done. Our new home was well planned, comfortable and convenient. The parts still unfinished when we moved in were completed later. Piped for running water and wired for electricity, the house was livable even in its unfinished state. It had three bedrooms, a bath, a kitchen and a living room with a stone fireplace. And there just off the living room was my "suggestion," a den. To add to the surprise, behind the door were built-in bookshelves with three spacious drawers underneath, an amazing little room. We placed Earl's desk between the two windows, the sewing machine on one side and the typewriter on the other. There was even space for a small desk for

Mary Alden.

As it turned out, Earl himself benefited as much as anyone from the den. Somewhat removed from the rest of the house, it afforded quiet and freedom from distraction when he had deskwork to do. Small as it was, it fulfilled the purpose for which it was intended, keeping clutter and disorder out of the living room.

The rest of the house was equally remarkable. Later Earl paneled with birch the walls of the living room, den, kitchen and hall and put a good finish on the oak floors. All the rooms were of good size and had plenty of light. Through large windows we looked out to the woods, the lake and the moving stream. The outlet was part of the place. The sound of its waters was in our ears by day whenever we stepped outside. In the silence of the night we could hear it flowing over the dam at the bridge. We named it ByBrook.

We had not been in our new home very long before Earl's building services were again in demand. Mr. Fred Rosenau of Fourth Lake had an architect's plan for a camp that he wished Earl to build. Crippled though he was, Earl agreed.

By fall the building was well started, and by early winter he had completed the outside walls, the roof and the living room fireplace. Leaving one or two men to work inside through the winter while he was in Florida, he was able to complete the job on his return in the spring. The Rosenaus were much pleased with their new camp, and for several years afterward Earl received from them a large fruitcake as a Christmas gift.

From then on Earl did little building in the North. The months in Florida, from October each year until May or June, left no time for more than short summer jobs in Big Moose. As time passed the arthritic pain and lameness eased somewhat, but it definitely had a slowing-up effect. Earl was beginning to slacken his pace. That did not mean, however, that he had stopped building entirely. We were spending a considerable part of our time in Florida, and we expected to have a home there. Earl was determined to build it.

Building in Florida

When we returned for our second winter in the South we realized that our rather hasty purchase the preceding year was not altogether satisfactory, and so we decided to sell the lot and look for another, now that we had time to drive around and look more carefully.

One day as we were driving through the Crest Lake section of Clearwater, where development was just beginning, we noticed land to the east of the park, which surrounded the lake. It was a quiet area. That part of Cleveland Street had very few homes and very little traffic. As we drove along the west side of the park we looked across to the vacant lots on the opposite side. We could visualize a home there, facing the park and the lake, with a view of sunsets like those we remembered at Clearwater Beach the year before. Before we left for the North that spring, we purchased the lots across the entire west end of the block east of Crest Lake Park. This time we had made no mistake.

We had an ideal spot for our Florida home. Once again Earl became absorbed in building work, as plans for another house began to take shape. This helped to take his mind off the aches and pains that had so sorely afflicted him of late.

For a long time, even before the Chapel was finished, he wanted to build a stone house. Having learned that there were quarries in Elberton, Georgia, not far away, he made up his mind that our Clearwater house should be built of stone. He proposed that on our way north in 1939 we drive to Elberton to arrange for a shipment from a granite quarry there, to be delivered to Clearwater in the fall.

It was the following January before we were able to return to Florida for the winter, but with the arrival of a shipment of Elberton stone soon afterward, work on our house began. Georgia granite is easier to work than the very hard variety that is quarried in the Adirondacks, and with several men on the job the cutting and laying of the stone proceeded without difficulty. By spring the house was ready, and before we left Florida for Big Moose in May 1940, we had moved and were comfortably settled in.

It was a beautiful place, in the strength of its cut stone and the

The Later Years

Earl Covey built his first house at 1 South Lake Drive in Clearwater, Florida in 1939-1940. Built with Georgia granite it was distinctive and boasted an interior reminiscent of popular construction styles in the Adirondacks. The stone fireplace, beamed ceilings and pine paneling were just what Earl thought a home should have.

simplicity of its design. Soon it was surrounded by full-grown palm and citrus trees, which Earl brought and set in the yard. It was as though house, trees and everything had always been there.

The interior was just as beautiful. The living room with its pine paneling, beamed ceiling open to the rafters and stone fireplace was Earl's idea of what a living room in that kind of a house should be. The bedrooms, each in a light, harmonizing color, were in delicate contrast to the woodwork of the living room and kitchen.

The house was completely satisfying in every way — in appearance and in the manner in which it had been planned for family living. Beyond all of this, we had our view to the west. There were the park, the little lake and the sunsets. For more than ten years Earl had dreamed of a place like this. His dream was realized. He had his stone house at last.

The changes that occurred in 1938, leasing Covewood and going to Florida, had their continuing effect on subsequent events. At the expiration of his lease Walter Reid decided not to exercise his first option to buy. Earl sold the property to Gladys Bourner, a former guest. The closing on the sale was early in 1942.

It was not easy to let Covewood go. But the real wrench for Earl had been in 1938 when the lease was first granted to Walter Reid. Since then more than three years had passed. Florida's climate had improved Earl's health. He had a home there, and he was looking forward to some building activity under the easier conditions afforded by living in the South. Covewood was part of his past.

Mary Alden, Student at Northfield

Winters in Florida, while beneficial to Earl, proved somewhat of a problem to our daughter, now a student in senior high school. After being in a Florida school the greater part of the academic year, she was finding it difficult to return to school in the North for just a short time before taking the June examinations under the New York State Board of Regents. It became necessary to decide whether she should complete her education in the North or in the South. She had little enthusiasm for Florida, either for living or for school there.

It had long been my wish that she might attend the girls' school in East Northfield, Massachusetts, where I had done my college preparatory work. I felt sure that she would benefit from its high ideals and its standards of scholarship, which I myself had found so helpful. Somewhat hesitantly I broached the subject to Earl, explaining why I thought Mary Alden should apply for admission to Northfield.

The idea was difficult for Earl to accept at first. As he gave it more thought, however, and became aware of the advantages to Mary Alden in being in a school like Northfield, he finally gave his consent. She applied for admission for the fall term of 1942. In acknowledging the application the school advised us that we would be notified during the summer whether or not her application had been accepted.

Shortly after mid-August the word arrived. Owing to the number of applications "more urgent," than hers, there would not be room on the campus that fall for Mary Alden.

Unwilling to take No for an answer, I decided to pursue the matter further. I wrote to the school, asking if she would be accepted if we could find a place for her off campus, in a private home. The reply was not positive. Such an arrangement had been tried in the past and found unsatisfactory. In desperation, I wrote again. If we, her parents, came with her to Northfield to live, could she enter the school as a day student?

To that the answer was Yes.

Relieved as I was to learn of this possibility, I realized that it was only a possibility. Earl might not even consider it. I summoned the courage to tell him of the word I had received from Northfield. He replied with a quaver in his voice, "I'm afraid if we do that we won't get to Florida." I assured him as confidently as I could that we should not have to give up Florida. It was more than likely that the school would have a vacancy at the beginning of the second term. That would make room for Mary Alden on campus, and we could leave for the South.

Earl gave his consent, as he had to her application a few months earlier. It was an exceedingly difficult decision for him to make. I was asking a great deal. But our daughter, a girl in her middle teens, was going to be a long way from home. She should be in a school where she would receive good preparation for college and would also be under the right influences, such as we knew Northfield would provide. Earl considered it all and made his decision accordingly.

With the matter settled, the first thing to do, having notified the school of our intention to live in Northfield, was to find a house or apartment in the town, which we could rent for the time we were there. And so, about a week before the beginning of the fall term, we drove to Northfield to look for a place.

We found an apartment at the rear of the Bronson Inn,[1] owned and operated at the time by Dr. George Bronson, a retired clergyman. Our errand accomplished, we returned to Big Moose to complete preparations for the move. One day Earl said, giving me a

---

[1.] On Main Street in Northfield, Massachusetts. Originally a hotel, it was later a school (1829-1843), known as the Northfield Academy of Useful Knowledge. Dwight L. Moody, nineteenth-century evangelist and founder of the Northfield Schools, attended school there as a boy.

quick look, "I won't be able to go to Northfield with you, I have work here to finish."

This was a surprise and disappointment. I knew that he still had work to do at the lake, but I had hoped that he might be with us in Northfield for the fall and early winter. With plans made for Mary Alden to enter school in Northfield it seemed best for me to go with her. Earl would join us as soon as his work allowed, but he agreed to help us with the move.

Knowing that we would need a place for stove wood, Earl built a woodbox to fit into the kitchen. The day came for our departure, and Earl loaded our things onto the truck. Along with the new woodbox he added the living room rug, which he thought we should have. It took the better part of a day to get to Northfield. When we arrived, the truck was unloaded and our things soon put in place.

Earl looked around until he found a farmer in Vermont who had stove wood to sell. After purchasing a load, he brought it back and deposited it in our back yard. Then, after he had done what he could to make us comfortable, he bade us good-bye and started on his way back to Big Moose where he would spend three months alone.

Through that time his daily routine was much the same. Up in the morning, breakfast, off to work, back at night, supper and then to bed. One day while at work he somehow became entangled in the extension cord of his electric saw and fell, injuring his knee. This, added to the arthritis, which continued to trouble him, caused great pain. But he worked until the job was done. It was mid-December before he could join us in Northfield.

There followed a month of waiting, until the end of the school term in January before we would know whether there would be a vacancy on campus. It gave Earl time to rest and become better acquainted with Dr. Bronson. It was not long before the two became warm friends. Dr. Bronson greatly admired our good-looking woodbox, its low, curved arms at each end giving it the appearance of a long seat.

In their conversations the doctor expressed to Earl his wish to give the building added protection from the cold. December and

January had been unusually severe. Could Earl build a vestibule at the front entrance to help keep the place warm?

The doctor got his vestibule. Working much of the time in a piercing wind, Earl finished the task at about the same time that we received word of a vacancy at the school. A room was open and available for Mary Alden on the campus.

As soon as we saw her settled in East Gould Hall we loaded the truck and departed for Big Moose with the things we had brought to Northfield. We left the load at the house and were on our way out of the northern cold and bound for the Florida sunshine. One thing we did not take from the Northfield apartment was the woodbox. We left that in the kitchen.

Each time we returned to Northfield, Earl made a point of seeing Dr. Bronson, and the two men would always enjoy a good visit. The good doctor would always express his gratitude to Earl for the vestibule. On one of those visits he took us up to the old ballroom on the top floor. There, to our surprise, against the wall at one side of the room was Earl's woodbox. Raising the lid, Dr. Bronson proudly displayed the contents. There were the sermons he had written during the years of his active ministry, placed in the box for safekeeping.

Summers at Twitchell Lake

With Mary Alden in Northfield we were able to continue our winters in Florida. But our summers for a few years were to be somewhat different from those of the past.

During the early 1930's, after Sumner Covey and his family had left Twitchell Lake to live in Clinton, New York, there were a few seasons of changing management at the Inn. Finally Earl sold the property to Mrs. Mary Boardman and her partner Samuel Blake Jr. Later Blake purchased Mrs. Boardman's interest, and during World War II he and his wife, Frances, were its owners. With the entrance of the United States into the war, Sam Blake, as a family man, was offered the choice between active military service and work in a defense plant. He chose the latter, but even though he did not have to leave the States, his defense work left him little time to be at the

Inn. Frances would have to assume responsibility there.

Knowing that it would be next to impossible for her to carry on alone, Earl volunteered to do what he could to help in Sam's absence. And so it came about that for three summers during the War Earl was at Twitchell instead of at home on Big Moose Lake. Eventually all three of us were at the Inn, engaged in various tasks.

Earl spent most of his first summer at Twitchell coaxing along a worn-out generator plant for making electricity. It would stop running without a moment's warning and at the most inopportune times. Mechanics from near and far came to work on it, sometimes way into the night. Even when it did run it had to be watched. Night after night Earl sat tending the unpredictable generator until eleven o'clock, at which time the line was switched to a smaller plant to operate until morning. It was a great relief to everyone when a new daytime plant finally replaced the old one. It was during those hours of watching, in the little shed that housed the electric-light plant above the Inn, that Earl wrote "A Woodsman's Prayer." [See page 166.] That is the prayer inscribed on the memorial plaque at the Big Moose Chapel.

One of Frances Blake's wartime problems at the Inn was that of keeping on hand a sufficient supply of meat. Meat was rationed and difficult to obtain. Now and then Earl would drive away in his car and be gone all day. On his return the beef and lamb in the cooler of the Inn were noticeably replenished. Whenever the supply dwindled there was another trip out of the woods and again the cooler was filled. This continued as long as meat rationing lasted.

We also had turkey for dinner on Sunday. When in amazement people asked Earl how he knew where to find the birds, he would say with a smile, "I had a dream."

At first I thought he was joking, but after I heard him give the same answer repeatedly, my curiosity was aroused. What did he mean, a "dream"? He explained that on one of his hunting trips to Canada he had seen turkeys sitting on rail fences by the roadside. In his dream he approached a town that looked like Westernville, New York, near Syracuse. There he saw a row of turkeys perched on a fence.

Shortly afterward, when Frances wished to serve turkey at the

Inn, Earl decided to go see what he could find. He drove directly to Westernville, and there, not on a fence but on a farm near the village of his dream, he found the turkeys. From then on guests at Twitchell Lake Inn had turkey for Sunday dinner.

This was not all that Earl did during his wartime summers at Twitchell. Besides the care of the light plant, the many journeys out of the woods for provisions and occasionally trips to meet the early morning train, there were square dances to plan for. Earl had to arrange with Jermaine Mitchell in Forestport for the music and with Barney Lepper, the local station agent, for help with the calling. Last but not least, he had to let everyone in the vicinity know there was to be a party. To see Earl on the night of the square dance, as agile and graceful as in the days of his youth, one would never suspect that he had just taken four aspirin tablets to relieve the arthritic ache and stiffness after a long busy day. Now past the age of sixty-five, he was still very much the "life of the party."

Always busy, he had little time to spend talking. It was seldom that one could hold him up long enough for a visit. Once, however, the guests persuaded him to spend an evening telling stories of life in the woods as he recalled it from his own long experience. They cherished the memory of that evening with him.

During the summer of 1945, in observance of the twentieth anniversary of the opening of Covewood, Miss Bourner gave a square dance party to which the Coveys were invited. She asked Dr. Percy Wightman, long a summer resident at Big Moose Lake, to say a few words during the intermission. In his speech he graciously paid tribute to Covewood and to Covewood's builder. The guests applauded. Then, turning to Earl, they called "Speech! Speech!"

Totally unprepared for such a demonstration, Earl hesitated. After some urging he stepped out from the group he had joined as Dr. Wightman was talking. He spoke briefly but in words so well chosen and with such dignity and poise that his response would have done credit to any experienced speaker. This and the evening of reminiscences with guests at Twitchell Inn were the only times I ever knew him to speak in public.

The season of 1945 was Earl's last summer of wartime service at Twitchell. During the following year the Inn again changed hands, this time going back to members of the Covey family, Earl's daughter, Mildred, and her husband, Fayette Brownell. With the War over, and knowing that the Brownells could carry on the business, Earl was free to turn his attention to other matters. His work at the Inn during those crucial years had enabled the Blakes to keep the place going. This helped them immeasurably, but it also afforded him the opportunity to make his own contribution to the War effort. He did "his bit" faithfully and well.

Our Second Florida Home

While, like everyone else, we were affected by wartime conditions, we were not obliged to greatly alter our way of life. We continued our trips to and from Florida. When gasoline under the rationing system was not available for the family car, we traveled two years by bus. After that we went in Earl's truck. Trucks were allowed more gasoline than passenger automobiles. The truck was more comfortable than a bus, and it provided a means of transportation for material that, despite wartime shortages, Earl was getting together for another house.

Clearwater entered a period of rapid growth. Homes were in demand, and prices were going up. Earl had not much more than finished our home on the northwest corner of South Lake Drive when he looked toward his southwest corner and wished he could build a house there. The lot was part of his purchase in 1939, and it was a very desirable location. Consequently, when someone was ready to buy our first Clearwater house Earl took advantage of the opportunity, sold at a profit and by the fall of 1943 was ready to start building a second house on his other corner of South Lake Drive.

Wartime regulations limited the amount of new material that could be used, and there was a ceiling on the over-all cost of new homes. Earl fortunately had on hand enough lumber to make his own door and window frames, which he took to Florida from Big Moose. He made two trips that fall, each with a load of material. Wherever he was, in the North or the South, he was constantly on the lookout for building supplies some of which he purchased new,

The second house in Florida was built near the first at 9 South Lake Drive. It was a period of rapid growth in Clearwater, and the Coveys had no difficulty selling the first house. Like the first, this house was built with granite from Georgia and had knotty pine paneling, a stone fireplace and a lovely view. The Coveys moved in in 1944.

some secondhand.

One time he was much impressed by a double sink that he saw in a Boonville store. It was a good unit but expensive. He did not buy it, but he came home and told me about it. With a little encouragement he would have gone back to buy it.

There were government restrictions and all the other costs in the building of the house. Wouldn't a less expensive sink do as well for the time being? We could install a better one later. Thus I reasoned with Earl, and reluctantly, he agreed.

Fixtures for the bathroom had to be found. One day he saw half dozen complete sets in the Old Forge Hardware and Furniture Store. He told the proprietor he would buy one of them.

"Oh, I can't let you have it," was the reply. "Those are all going to Blue Mountain Lake."

"But I've got to have it." And, to use one of his own expressions, Earl "stuck and hung" until finally the proprietor yielded. There was nothing else he could do. He would tell the Blue Mountain customer the shipment was short one set, and he would try to get another. When Earl left the store that day one of the fixture sets went with him.

Despite the difficulties of building in wartime, our second Clearwater home, begun in 1943, was ready for us by the following spring. It was not quite finished. Flooring ordered for the guest room had not arrived, and the stonework on the outside, which was to be like that on the other house, remained to be done. But after a winter in an uncomfortable apartment we were only too glad to be in a home of our own, unfinished as it was.

It was a lovely house, just right for two people. The living room in particular, with knotty pine walls, a stone fireplace and a view of the park across the way, was a constant comfort and delight. Closer to the lake than we had been before, farther from traffic yet convenient to the main highway the location suited us perfectly.

Ventures Into Real Estate

In addition to the lots on South Lake Drive, Earl made two other ventures into Florida real estate. One was successful, the other was not. The latter, a fifty-five-acre citrus grove, was about four miles east of Clearwater. When he made the purchase, late in 1945, he planned to have Sumner Covey, living at the time in Florida, operate and eventually own the grove, which Earl thought would pay for itself in a few years. He did not realize that the inflated prices the government paid growers for their fruit were "for the duration" only. Once the War ended the government would not renew its contracts with citrus growers.

The postwar drop in the market price was so great as to rule out all prospects of immediate profit to Earl from his grove. By much hard work on Sumner's part, while Earl found ways to meet payments on the place as they came due, the two men managed to keep the grove in operation for a few years. Finally the land was divided and sold off in parcels to be developed for home sites. Thus ended Earl's first and last experience with a citrus grove.

The other venture was the purchase, in the late 1940's, of the block of vacant land just south of our house. Its west end faced the park, as did that of the block in which we lived. Earl was quick to see its possibilities for development. He made the acquaintance of the owner, an elderly man by the name of William Gibson, and expressed his interest in buying the property.

At first Mr. Gibson did not seem inclined to sell. But he liked Earl, and when he later decided to dispose of his holdings, knowing that Earl was anxious to have it, Mr. Gibson offered to sell the entire block at a reasonable price.

Earl accepted the offer without hesitating. There might not be an immediate demand for lots in the Crest Lake area, he thought, but the city was growing rapidly in that direction. He would hold the property and wait.

He did not have to wait long. Soon people began buying Earl's lots. In a surprisingly short time he had sold the last of some twenty in the block. That was a highly successful venture. Actually, it was not a venture, really. It was a "sure thing" from the start, and Earl knew it.

Along with the two houses for himself Earl did some building for others in Clearwater. He built an addition to Mrs. Mary Boardman's Garden Seat Tearoom, and he built a house for his young friend, Henry Blanton. Henry, about to marry, was making plans for a home. He had wished for a long time that he might have a house built by Mr. Covey. When Henry acquired a lot beside ours, Earl agreed to build for him. When the house was finished Henry and his bride moved in, very happy to be in their new little home.

There were small jobs, which Earl did to help friends and neighbors. Someone's fireplace smoked. Earl remedied that. A neighbor needed new bookshelves. Could Mr. Covey build them? A friend who had sought in vain for someone to repair a cherished photograph frame appealed to Earl for help. He mended the frame for her. A young man needed help on a chimney for his new house. Earl helped him build it. When he was not building or helping someone build he was taking one of his precious roses to a neighbor or shipping baskets of oranges and grapefruit to family and friends in the North. He was always thinking of what he could do for other people.

A House for Hassie Mae

And then there was Hassie Mae. From the time we had a home in Clearwater Hassie Mae Wright had been our faithful helper. She was like a member of the family. From the minute she stepped through the door in the morning, I knew that I could be free from all household cares for the rest of that day. Hassie Mae would take care of everything and do everything beautifully. She was clean, quiet and efficient, and her services were in such demand that she could pick and choose the families for whom she worked. We were fortunate to have her for the one day a week she gave us.

Hassie Mae had one great desire, a home for herself and her two children, whom she supported by working out by the day. Her husband had never adequately provided for the family, and she finally divorced him. She was paying too much rent for a rundown house in the Negro section, and she kept talking about a home of her own. She began to wonder if Mr. Covey could help her, and finally she mustered the courage to ask. Earl promised to do something for her as soon as he had time. He still had the stonework, much of which he did himself, to finish on our house. That would take several months. But he did not forget his promise to Hassie Mae.

Although we spent much of our time in Florida, it was our plan from the beginning to return to New York each summer. During Mary Alden's years at Northfield and in college she had vacation jobs at Twitchell Lake Inn and at Covewood. The former was within easy driving distance from ByBrook, and the latter was just across the outlet. Thus it was possible for us to keep in touch with each other through the summer months.

There were two summers, however, when Earl remained in Florida instead of going north. The first was in 1946, after he had purchased the grove. Realizing that there would be no profit from the sale of fruit at the prevailing low prices, he decided to stay in Florida through the summer in the hopes that he could sell the property. He thought he would have a better chance of making a sale if he stayed instead of being gone all summer. And so he stayed.

It was hard to go and leave Earl alone. However, it did not seem feasible for Mary Alden to make the trip south, owing to the expense and the lack of job opportunities for her in the Clearwater area. Further I did not think it was wise for her to be alone in the North through the long vacation without having one of us with her.

In 1948 Earl spent a second summer in Florida to complete the stonework on our house. When he learned that Henry and Annabelle Blanton were planning a trip to Annabelle's home in Pennsylvania, he urged them to drive on up to Big Moose. Because he could not be there to entertain them himself, he mailed me a check with a note to "give them a good time." Although their stay was brief, only two days, the Blantons seemed to enjoy the visit as much as Mary Alden and I enjoyed having them.

It was late September, after Mary Alden had gone back to college, before I could leave for the South. Earl had written early in the month asking when I expected to return. At the time I attached no particular significance to his query. It seemed only natural that he should wonder when I would be back after I had been gone all summer. As soon as I took Mary Alden to Geneva, New York, for the opening of William Smith College I went on my way. In a few days I was back in Clearwater.

It was only then that I learned why Earl had written to ask when I would return. He had suffered what was probably a slight stroke. The doctor had ordered him to rest, and for two weeks Sumner stayed with him at night. Earl's letter to me had not given the slightest inkling of anything wrong. By the time I reached Clearwater, he had apparently recovered and was back at work. We were thankful and relieved that his illness was no more serious.

Despite this interruption, with Sumner's help Earl finished our stonework that summer. Then the two men were ready to begin work on the house for Hassie Mae. First a lot had to be purchased. Hassie Mae did not have the ready cash, and so Earl advanced her the money to pay for it. Further he advised her to acquire an additional adjoining lot for protection, and with his help she purchased that, too.

By the spring of 1949 her house was finished. It had a living room, a kitchen, two bedrooms and a bath. It was equipped with running water and electricity. A comfortable little home, it was the first to be built in that neighborhood in a long time. It marked a beginning, at least, of better housing for Negroes in that community, for soon there followed two more new houses close by.

There were no set terms for payment. Earl's price was very reasonable, and Hassie Mae paid as she was able, bringing money to Earl on the days she came to work. She noticed that he seemed eager for her to move in and be settled before he left for Big Moose that summer. At last, her dream realized, Hassie Mae had a home of her own.

Wedding in the Family

We returned north in time for the William Smith College commencement in June 1949, an important occasion for us because it was the time of Mary Alden's graduation. In addition we were to meet her fiancé for the first time. They were to receive their diplomas, she from William Smith College and he from Hobart, at the joint exercises of the two colleges in Geneva, New York.

It was a happy experience for all of us. Young John Williams proved to be the kind of man we were glad to have our daughter marry, and as soon as commencement was over they began to make plans for a summer wedding. They decided to be married in August, which would give them time to be settled at the Mount Hermon School for Boys before Jack began his work teaching there in September.

Earl did not have to concern himself with wedding details, but there was something else on his mind. Jack and Mary Alden had no car. How were they going to get along without one?

Earlier in the summer, while on a visit to my old home in Connecticut, we learned that my mother was waiting for a new car, which had been ordered some time before. Deliveries at the time were very slow. It seemed to Mother that she had been waiting a terribly long time. One day a few weeks later Earl saw in a salesroom in Warrensburg, New York, the very model Mother had ordered.

That night he called her from Big Moose. Would she like Earl to get for her the car he had seen in Warrensburg? Yes, she replied, she would.

She canceled her original order. Earl made the purchase in Warrensburg, and shortly thereafter we all drove to Connecticut to deliver Mother's new car.

Upon discovering that the new lower-hung model made getting in and out more difficult, Earl built a stool, which Mother used to step in and out of the car when she went for a ride. I was never quite sure which delighted her more, the new car or that little stool. She never ceased to be grateful to Earl for this thoughtfulness for her comfort.

He also took care of the registration of the new Pontiac. As for the old one ... somehow Mother learned that Mary Alden and Jack, about to be married, had no car. The upshot of it was that on our return to Big Moose the Coveys were driving two cars. One was our own, and the other was Mother's old car, now re-registered in her granddaughter's name. And that solved the car problem for the soon to be bride and the groom.

As the August 20 date of the wedding drew near, some reference was made to a honeymoon. Jack had friends on Cape Cod whom he and Mary Alden had thought of visiting before going to Mount Hermon in September.

Then Earl remembered Brantingham Lake. Why would that not be a good place for their honeymoon? When Mary Alden seemed interested in her father's suggestion, he proposed a trip to Brantingham to see what the place had to offer.

A few days later we all drove to the lake and had lunch at the Inn. Interestingly, it was near the site of the Sunday School picnics of Earl's boyhood. After our lunch we started out to look for a camp to rent.

We found one on a rise overlooking the lake, at some distance from its neighbors. Of those we saw this seemed the most satisfactory. Earl put the question to Mary Alden. Would this be all right? When she agreed Earl engaged the camp for a week beginning with the day of the wedding, paid the rent then and there, and that settled the matter of the honeymoon.

Mary Alden had not expected to make the decision so quickly and without Jack's knowledge and consent. But she realized, soon after we had begun looking around at the lake, that her father wanted her and Jack to be at Brantingham. She did not have the heart to object. On several occasions in the past Earl had made one of his resort cottages available to newlyweds of his acquaintance, and now he was doing it for his own young people. He knew nothing about Cape Cod. Brantingham Lake, on the other hand, he had known since he was a boy. His wedding present to Mary Alden and Jack had to be connected with a place he knew, and that place was Brantingham.

The day of the wedding was a clear, sunny afternoon. It was perfect, as a wedding day should be. The Chapel, decorated with green boughs, was never more beautiful. The bride was a vision in white as she came down the aisle on her father's arm. The wedding music, the joyous meeting of friends afterward on the lawn to congratulate the bride and groom and the informal reception at Twitchell Lake Inn were wonderful. Everything was so perfect and so beautiful that it seemed no time for tears not even for Earl, who had dreaded the moment he would give his daughter away in marriage.

Mary Alden and Jack were on their way to Brantingham Lake. They had a car to take them there, and when they returned he would see them again. Mary Alden had married a fine man. That, after all, was what mattered most.

For the guests the wedding and the reception ended the day's festivities. But for the immediate families there was still something in store. My sister and her husband were staying overnight with us, and Earl purchased a lake trout for supper. Preparations for the meal were underway when Jack's parents and two cousins stopped on their way home to say good-bye. We persuaded them to stay and join us for supper.

With Earl's usual generous provision, what he had planned for four proved sufficient for eight. Against the rocks along the shore in front of the house, he built a fire for broiling. As he left the kitchen to grill the fish he called out, "Have everything ready when I come back." This meant having a space clear where he could set the broiler on returning it hot from the fire, a platter for the fish, butter to spread on it and plates for serving.

Given our orders, my sister and I did as we were told, and when Earl hurried back with the fish broiled to a turn, he served our guests a meal they would never forget. For all of us, that supper, unique in the manner of its cooking and serving and remarkable for the skill and dispatch with which it was done, made a perfect ending to an already perfect day.

After their honeymoon at Brantingham Lake the young Williamses went on to Cape Cod, where they spent a day or two before going finally to Mount Hermon. Shortly afterward we saw them settled in their first home. It was an apartment over the school gymnasium. When we made the trip we had with us some bookshelves and a kitchen cabinet, which Earl had built for them.

Chapter IX

Earl's Failing Health

We returned to Florida early in October of 1949. The house had had very little cleaning during our absence. We arrived, shortly after midday and found rugs and walls covered with cobwebs. It took the two of us working though the afternoon to get enough of the place cleaned so that we could begin unpacking. The following day Hassie Mae came to help, and while she and Earl washed windows I finished unpacking. By night the house was in order.

It was not yet daylight the next morning when I was suddenly aroused by a strange sound from Earl's bed. Perhaps he had tried to speak. I awoke to see that he was sitting up. Springing up and turning on the light, I was at his side as he tried to get up and on his feet. By holding him I prevented his falling but could not keep him from slipping off the bed to the floor. He lay there unable to raise himself. Placing a pillow under his head I rushed to the telephone to call our neighbor, who was Chief of the Clearwater Fire Department and an expert in first aid. He came immediately. Seeing Earl on the floor, he told me to call the doctor. In a matter of minutes the doctor arrived. He determined it to be a paralytic stroke. After administering medication to prevent hemorrhage he telephoned the hospital to have a bed ready then called an ambulance.

Earl protested at being taken from the house. "What's going on here?" he asked feebly.

For the next eight days he had to lie in bed to allow his brain time to heal after the damage caused by the ruptured blood vessel. It

Earl's Failing Health

was an ordeal, "slow murder" as Earl told the doctor and nurses. He wanted his clothes so that he could get up and go home. That was all he could talk about. All of us, doctor, nurses and family, kept telling him that he would be allowed to go home as soon as it was safe for him to do so.

Despite the fact that he was unhappy at having to stay in the hospital, there was one time when his sense of humor helped to relieve the situation. In the course of the various tests and analyses given the patients, one of the technicians, an unusually attractive young woman, came to Earl's bedside.

"I should like to take a sample of your blood, Mr. Covey," she said.

Something within Earl responded to the dark eyes, the lovely smile. "You can't wring blood out of a stone," was his quick reply.

Totally unprepared for such an answer, Henrietta Mathers had to regain her composure before she could obtain the sample.

Finally after eight days the doctor permitted his patient to leave the hospital to Earl's immeasurable relief. He could hardly wait to be home again. During the first weeks of his convalescence he rested, part of the time in bed and part of the time sitting by the living-room window or on the porch. He could look from there out to the park, see the highway traffic in the distance and at the end of the day watch the sunset. Now and then he went for a ride.

Earl's recovery was gradual. The doctor thought he would continue to improve over the next two years. Little by little he began regaining use of his left arm and leg. He began trying to use his tools. Unaccustomed as he was to physical weakness Earl and his naturally cheerful and buoyant spirit were put to a severe test. But he persevered. His will to recover contributed in no small measure to the return of his physical strength.

During the months that followed Earl resumed some activity. The house at the grove had been moved back from the road and was being remodeled. Plans included the installation of a new bathroom. In order to complete the "roughing in" on the drainpipes, Earl, smaller than the others, crawled under the building and finished the job, only to discover that he did not have the strength to crawl out again. Someone had to crawl in and pull him from under the house. But the roughing in was accomplished.

It was at about this time that people began to show interest in the lots Earl had acquired from Mr. Gibson. Earl welcomed the opportunity to meet and talk with prospective buyers. Without being too arduous this kept him interested and occupied and was of benefit to him both physically and mentally. The stroke had weakened and further slowed him up, but he was not ready to quit. He still had work to do.

Hillis Miller

One of the happy experiences of Earl's later years was his renewed friendship with Hillis Miller, who since serving as summer minister at Big Moose had won distinction in the field of higher education.

From teaching and administrative work at Bucknell University, to the presidency of Keuka College, to the office of Associate Commissioner of Education for the State of New York and finally to the University of Florida, he had been a long way. In the spring of 1947 he was called to the presidency of the University of Florida, and we received an invitation to the inauguration. Even though he knew Hillis would have no time to see him that day, Earl wanted to attend, and he decided we should go.

We were both glad we went. From the beginning of the exercises, when the visiting dignitaries in colorful academic procession filed in to take their places, to the last words of the President's inaugural speech, Earl watched and listened attentively. As Hillis delivered his address to the more than two thousand people, he moved from one side of the platform to the other, the more easily to maintain rapport with his audience. Having outlined his plan of development for the University, he stepped to the center of the platform, and facing the entire assembly he concluded by saying, "Finally, I hope to see on this campus a beautiful chapel, erected to the honor and glory of Almighty God."

For an instant Hillis' closing words brought back memories of Big Moose Chapel, of the years Hillis was there. It was as if he had spoken to the Coveys, no one else. On the way home that after-

Earl's Failing Health

noon, our minds filled with all that we had seen and heard, we drove for a time in silence. Earl was the first to speak. "I wish I could help Hillis with that chapel," he said.

Three years passed. As president of the University of Florida, Hillis Miller traveled the length and breadth of the state, meeting as many people as time permitted, to make known his plans for the University and to enlist their support. His personality and convincing manner won him many friends, and he was in demand as a speaker all over the state.

Early in 1950 he was to address a public meeting in Clearwater. Earl very much wanted to see him but was convalescing from his illness at the time and did not feel able to attend the meeting. We decided that I should go and afterward see Hillis to ask if he could stop at the house for a visit with Earl before returning to Gainesville.

Hillis was glad for the opportunity. He was to stay overnight in Clearwater, and that gave him some free time in the evening. As soon as the public meeting was over we drove to the house, where Earl was waiting. I had prepared Hillis for any change he might notice in his old friend, and from the moment he entered the room with his hearty "Hello" until he left not a word was said about the illness. It was as if it had not been. The two men picked up where they had left off when they last saw each other. They had an hour together. Hillis did most of the talking. Earl listened eagerly with affectionate pride in the younger man's notable achievement since the days when they worked and planned for the Chapel at Big Moose.

Change had come with the passing of time. Instead of the Big Moose Chapel, Hillis' primary interest was the University of Florida. The differences in the two men twenty years before was even more apparent. Hillis was at the height of his career. Earl was frail and aging. His work all but done. But just as the difference had not mattered then, no more did it matter in our house in Florida. If anything, time had strengthened the bond between them.

"I wish I could help with that chapel, Hillis," Earl said.

"You can help with the president's house," was Hillis' reply. "It is going to be one of the most beautiful homes in the South." On this he could speak with assurance as the State had already appropriated funds for the house. His dream of a chapel on the University campus was yet to be realized.

When it came time for Hillis to go, he had Earl's promise that on our trip north in the spring we would go by way of Gainesville to see the Millers at their home. The evening was a red-letter event for Earl, and he began to look forward to seeing Hillis again within a few months before returning north.

On the day that we left Clearwater near the end of May, we reached Gainesville before noon to have lunch with the Millers. While Mrs. Miller was busy with preparations for the meal, Hillis took us around the University campus. We passed one new building after another. I finally exclaimed, "You must have been laying a cornerstone nearly every day."

In the three years Hillis had been president, the enrollment had increased from three thousand to ten thousand. There was so much he wanted Earl to see and so little time to see it. As it was, we were somewhat late for Mrs. Miller's luncheon of fried chicken and hot biscuits. After lunch the men went out to the front porch, where they sat and talked. Mrs. Miller and I visited for a while inside, later joining our husbands.

It was near mid-afternoon. We had had a happy reunion, brief though it was, and it was time for the Coveys to be going. To start us on our way, Hillis lead in his car until he reached the route we were to follow. Then, as he turned aside to let us pass, we all waved good-bye and drove on.

One of Earl's summer projects since the building of the Chapel had been that of helping with the annual Guides Supper. In the beginning he had done much of the hard work himself, from the setting up the tables to broiling the steak. Soon after our return to the lake in 1950 he was asked to help again, with the understanding that he was only to supervise. For Earl, supervising had always meant "pitching in," working harder than anyone else. For the first time, he was willing to let others do the heavy part. But he wanted to order the meat. He drove to Utica, made a selection from beef hanging in Armour's cooler and had it tagged with his name, to be called for in time for the supper.

Earl's Failing Health

Each year at the Guides Supper there seemed to be the problem of keeping food hot until it was served at the tables. Finally free from the more difficult and demanding tasks, Earl began to consider the means of keeping plates hot until ready for use. He devised a steel drum with a built-in shelf to be placed near the open fire as the meat was broiled. The plates, put there to be warmed, were so hot when removed that they could not be touched with bare hands. There were not many complaints of cold food at that supper.

Further Service to the Chapel

For a number of years the pointing up the mortar on the outside of the Chapel had been a cause of concern to the trustees. Not an immediate need at the time the building was first done, this work had been deferred until there were sufficient funds in the treasury for the purpose and until someone could be found for the job. When not busy at Big Moose Earl had been in Florida in recent years and was unavailable. The Trustees finally decided that the work should not be delayed any longer, and the chairman of the board asked Earl to find someone to do the pointing up. Earl thought of Louis Panunzio, his helper in cutting stone for the Chapel. He made a trip to Malone to see Panunzio only to find that the stonecutter was out of town on another job.

There seemed to be nothing for Earl to do but find local men to help him and work on the building himself. This, so soon after his stroke, seemed a risky undertaking. He would have to work on staging much of the time at a considerable height from the ground. But the job had to be done, and there was no one else to do it.

The pointing up, though not difficult, was tedious and time consuming. It took three men, working steadily, several weeks to finish. Sitting for hours with one's feet dangling from the staging would have been a test of endurance at best. For Earl, afflicted with arthritis, it was a painful ordeal. Finally to everyone's relief the last mortar was smoothed into place and the pointing up was complete.

Mrs. Vander Veer's Tribute

At the Communion Service held each summer at Big Moose Chapel, four men from the board of trustees assist in passing the elements of the communion. Earl was usually one of the four. While arranging for the 1950 service one of the trustees asked me if I thought Earl felt able to assist in view of his recent illness. Not sure whether he could hold the tray carrying the communion cups, I could not give a definite answer. And so our trustee friend put the question directly to Earl.

Earl decided that he could act in this capacity and was accordingly one of the four to assist at the service. He passed the elements in their order, first the plate of bread and then the heavier tray holding the communion cups with little if any difficulty just as he had often done in the past. Mrs. Edgar Vander Veer, long a summer resident at the lake who had known Earl for many years, afterward said to him, "It was a privilege to receive the Communion from you, Earl."

An incident occurred later summer that gave Mrs. Vander Veer's words added significance. Earl's great-granddaughter Virginia had sustained an injury to one of her eyes when a hen suddenly flew up and struck her. In order to save the good eye the injured one had to be removed. This necessitated her going to a hospital in Utica.

While she was still there Earl and I had errands, which took us to the city for a day. Because Earl had expressed his desire to go to the hospital before leaving Utica, we planned to drive there on the way home. I noticed that he mentioned it two or three times, which I attributed to the fact that I was driving and he wanted to make sure that I understood his request. It seemed only natural, and I thought nothing more about it at the time.

Accordingly, with our errands done, we drove to the hospital. Virginia's mother, Ruth, was there when we arrived, and it was Ruth whom Earl particularly wished to see. He had come to tell her that he was offering his eyes to Virginia. He did not have long to live, he said, and if Virginia could use his eyes he would like her have them.

All his life Earl had given freely to those in need. He had given his time, his strength and his means, sometimes at great cost to himself. But that was what he chose to do, and he did so gladly. He offered his eyes to Virginia.

Touched and deeply grateful, Ruth explained to her grandfather that such a sacrifice on his part would not be necessary. With an artificial eye, identical in appearance to the one that had been removed and with perfect vision in the other, Virginia would be able to lead a normal life once she recovered from the operation.

Assured that the accident would not affect Virginia seriously, Earl did not pursue the matter further. Virginia was able to leave the hospital shortly afterward, and with an artificial eye in place of the injured one, she was soon as well as ever.

Mrs. Vander Veer was right. It was a privilege to receive Communion at Earl's hands. Not knowing of his offer to Virginia, she had paid him a tribute, which he deserved even more than she knew.

Addition to the Florida House

On his return to Clearwater there remained one more task for Earl, the addition of a garage and breezeway to the house. For months he had been exercising his arms and hands in the use of stonecutting tools. Finally, with the chisel in his left hand and wielding the hammer with his right, he began to cut and lay stone. He had men to help with the work, and by the spring of 1951 the addition was complete.

The new part did more than provide needed living and garage space. It transformed the appearance of the entire house. The added length brought beauty of proportion to what had been just a block structure before. It enhanced the dignity and strength of the stone. It was more than an addition. It was a monument to the strength of will of its builder and to his determination to finish the task he had started.

Since his stroke in 1949 Earl's health had continued to improve. He had gone back to cutting stone. Meanwhile his physician had left Clearwater for a year of study, and Earl, not wishing to consult a stranger, had not had a medical checkup during that time. I began urging him to see a doctor. Finally he agreed upon our return north for the summer of 1951.

He had no particular plans while at Big Moose, other than to help with the Guides Supper in August. It was at about that time that the doctor decided to change the medication prescribed for Earl earlier in the summer. He thought that digitalis in a purer form might benefit his patient. Unfortunately it made Earl ill, and he was unable to attend the supper.

Keenly disappointed, he felt that he had let the congregation down, although his friends knew full well that his absence was not due to any lack of interest on his part. The doctor put him back on the original medication prescribed.

Although Earl had to miss the Guides Supper, he was able to do other things that summer. He remembered his mother's blackberry pickles, and he wanted to taste them once more. He asked his grandson Jim Brownell to take him and Jim's mother to Glenfield for blackberries and to find someone there who knew the recipe his mother used. He learned of a woman who had a similar recipe, and he arranged with her to make him a supply of the pickles. Even though they did not taste quite like his mother's, Earl had his blackberry pickles. Another time, hungry for homemade bread, he built a hot fire in the kitchen stove and baked a batch. It was good.

Mrs. Mary Boardman was our guest for a few weeks. While she was with us she expressed a desire to see Elk Lake, in the woods northwest of Schroon Lake. Part of the main highway was under construction, and the approach to the lake was over a narrow dirt road. But beautiful Elk Lake, once reached, made the hard trip worthwhile. On the way back we took a different route and enjoyed the drive home over a good road. Earl was glad for his day at Elk Lake.

Gladys Bourner sold Covewood Lodge to C. Vernon Bowes Jr., a young hotel man commonly known as the Major. After a successful season, the Major was considering an addition to the Lodge. This was to be a long structure consisting of about ten units, each with its own fireplace. He expressed the hope that Earl, from his own long experience, might give suggestions and advice. As the two men discussed the matter Earl became convinced that one way in which he could help was by saving the Major a considerable sum in the purchase of stone for the fireplaces. When we left Big Moose for

Florida in October of 1951 Earl was expecting to help the Major in an advisory capacity when it came time to build his addition.

Failing Health

On arriving in Clearwater we found that our physician had returned to his practice in the city thus making it possible for Earl to have the care he needed from someone he knew. As the doctor talked to Earl in the months that followed, he learned about the proposed building at Covewood and how Earl was going to save Major Bowes money buying stone.

A weakened heart, with resulting lung congestion, made breathing for Earl increasingly difficult. He tried sleeping in the breezeway, where there was good cross-ventilation. The cool night air may have helped, but he got very little sleep. His rest consisted mostly of brief naps. Sometimes he would go inside during the night, and in the morning I would find him sitting by the living room window wrapped in a blanket. As the time drew near for our return north for the summer, I asked the doctor if he thought Earl should make the trip. "I can't tell him he shouldn't go," was the reply.

No, the doctor could not. Not after he heard of the plans for the addition at Covewood and of the stone Earl would get for the fireplaces. The trip might shorten his life. He might not be able to help Major Bowes after he reached there. But if that was where he wanted to be the doctor would not stand in his way.

Often when taxes were due on the Clearwater property Earl declared they were too high and that he would sell the house. True, the city taxes were high, but I did not at first take his remarks seriously, thinking they reflected merely a passing mood. But the idea grew in his mind until by that spring he had listed the place with several realtors, hoping to sell before we left for the North. It took longer than that, however, because the house was not new. It had been built eight years before. Ultimately and ironically, the people who bought it preferred our house to some of the newer ones they had seen.

The night before we started for Big Moose our good family friends the Blantons came to say good-bye. They knew that Earl was far from well, and they wanted to see him before he left.

    We had a much more comfortable trip than we dared to hope for. The cooler air as we proceeded northward seemed to make his breathing easier. The changing landscape added interest and variety. On the day that we drove through Old Forge he had an appointment with the local physician, who from then on had Earl under his care.

Chapter X

Summer 1952

We arrived at Big Moose late in June on a Monday. After a week of unpacking and getting settled we were looking forward to the Chapel service scheduled for the following Sunday. By the end of the week the house was in order. On the next day we got ready for church and drove to the Chapel.

To our surprise no one was there. There was no service. We drove on to find out from a neighbor what had happened and were informed that the day was not Sunday but Saturday. In my desire to be settled for the summer as quickly as possible I had kept at the unpacking until I had completely lost track of time, and when by the end of the week I was ready to resume normal living I skipped a day. In annoyance at my miscalculation I exclaimed that the days were all alike with no way of telling one from another. To which Earl replied, "We'll have to cut notches in a stick."

Soon after our return to the lake our friends the MacMackins visited us over a weekend. While awaiting their arrival on Saturday afternoon, Earl and I were resting. I had dropped off to sleep. Earl heard their car as it drove into the yard. He was up, off the bed and down the hall, and by the time our guests appeared he was there to meet them with a cheery "Good afternoon, folks!" It was a greeting the MacMackins never forgot.

On examining Earl a week later the doctor found the heart muscle "very weak" and prescribed bed rest and the use of oxygen. But lying still in bed was difficult for Earl, and the oxygen afforded him only partial relief. After two days he was permitted to sit up part of the time, even to be out of bed. This may have been against the doctor's better judgment, but his first consideration was the patient's comfort.

The nights were long. Earl wondered if he could get more sleep on the porch. We agreed that it would be worth trying, and with the help of two boys who were employed at Covewood Lodge we began to get one end of the porch ready for his use. Earl was there to see how everything was going to be done.

A wire to hold a curtain had to be stretched across part of the porch where the bed was to be. One of the nails holding the wire was to be driven into the porch post. Earl wanted the nail to go in at an angle, which would tighten and straighten the wire as the nail was driven in. At first the boys did not know how to do this. Earl tried to explain. After seeing them make several unsuccessful attempts to drive the nail the way it should go, I began to wonder if it could not just as well go in some other way. I made some comment to that effect.

"There is a right way and a wrong way," was Earl's quick retort. "I'm trying to show them the right way." At that moment with a single blow from the hammer the wire tightened and straightened. The nail was in the right way.

After two nights on the porch and still unable to sleep, Earl decided to go back indoors. With his bed between two windows, and an electric fan to keep the air in motion, he found that he was as comfortable inside as anywhere.

I had been trying without success to find a housekeeper and a day nurse. We had a night nurse on duty since the early part of July. Finally I wrote to Mary Alden at Mount Hermon and asked if she could come and stay until I could find the necessary help. The whole family came, Mary Alden, Jack and their two young children. They were very helpful, and it cheered Earl to have them there. He also enjoyed an occasional glimpse of the little ones.

"Hello, Buckshot!" he would call out to his small grandson, not quite two years old, as the little fellow came trotting down the hall. Fortunately, at the time the Williamses had to leave, ten days later, an excellent male nurse arrived to take care of Earl.

As Earl lay in bed he could look out to Mrs. Milligan's camp next door. One day he saw a man painting her roof. The man was not a house painter by trade. He was a clergyman who, as a guest of Mrs. Milligan, was rendering her a service in this way. The work was going very slowly. Earl watched for a while. Finally he said, "I could show that man how to paint that roof in about a quarter of the time."

Seeing that Earl was becoming uneasy at the progress of the painting, I asked the clergyman-painter if he would be willing to come to the house and let Earl talk with him.

He came and received his directions. The paint should be poured from the can to a pail, and a long handle should be attached to the brush. The larger container would make dipping the brush much easier, and the lengthened handle would reach farther, covering the surface to be painted more quickly. By following the directions the amateur painter was able to accomplish the work in a much shorter time than otherwise would have been possible.

Although Earl had given up trying to spend his nights on the porch, for a while he was able to sit outside during the day where he could watch the activity along the South Bay shore. He could see people on their docks relaxing in the sunshine or swimming. He could watch an occasional boat or canoe going out from the shore and now and then hear the sound of voices or the noise of an outboard motor in the distance. All this was part of the life of the lake on a summer afternoon.

It was on a day such as that we sat looking out at the scene before us. There had been a few moments of silence. I said to Earl, "Of all the houses we have lived in, I like this the best." There was so much at ByBrook that the other houses did not have, the lake, the hills, the woods and there were friendships and memories associated with the house. To me, it was home.

"It is the loveliest place in the world," Earl replied.

And yet there were other thoughts in his mind as the days of summer passed. One afternoon as he walked down the hall on his way to the front porch I heard him say, "I wish I could go home … If I could only go home." I feel sure that Earl's mind was perfectly clear that he knew where he was and that he was at that moment where he most wanted to be in his own home on Big Moose Lake.

But life had become a burden. He longed for release.

There was little that he needed to do to put his affairs in order. That had already been done before his return to Big Moose. However, I know he had been thinking about our home at the lake. One day in the nurse's absence he wanted to talk about it. First he asked for a map showing the lots he owned, one on either side of the outlet. I was unable to find his map nor could I locate one in the vicinity.

Then he wanted to see Fred Brack. Fred came over that afternoon, and Earl talked with him about the boundaries of the two lots. At his request Fred promised to sometime show me where they were. That satisfied Earl, even though there was no map at hand to consult. He knew that Fred was familiar with the lot lines. Earl advised me to keep the property intact, rather than divide it into separate lots. He also told me that there were springs below the Covewood bridge, which would furnish water for the house should the existing supply prove inadequate.

He talked of something else that afternoon, my future plans. He thought I should have a house in Florida and someone with me as a companion. He even suggested someone, a friend he had known for many years. I had not been able to think that far ahead. At that point I could live but one day at a time. Because of Earl's condition, further planning for the future was out of the question.

Realizing however, that the friend he had in mind would not be free to go, I was fortunate in being able to think quickly of another whom I mentioned by name. Immediately Earl agreed that she would be just the person, and it would be "wonderful" if she could go with me to Florida. Satisfied with the proposed arrangement, he dismissed the matter, and we did not speak of it again.

For more than a year Earl had had the presentiment that he would not live much longer. Now, it seemed, he faced the fact directly. He wished to make sure, while he was able, that all his affairs were in order. I was faced with the fact that eventually I would have to go on without him. But it was helpful, even so, to know his thinking and to have the benefit of his judgment concerning the matters on his mind.

There were frequent visitors as long as Earl's physician permitted.

One was Dr. Albert Vander Veer Jr. It had been a long time since the two friends had seen each other. The doctor was in a reminiscent mood. "You carried some awfully heavy loads," he recalled.

"I wanted to do my part," was Earl's reply.

He had done his part. He had done it in carrying packs over the trails, in providing for the comfort and pleasure of those in his care, in responding many times to calls for help with courageous leadership, which inspired hope in a time of crisis, turning apparent defeat into final victory.

In all of this, in wanting to do his part, he had walked his Second Mile,[1] going far beyond the call of his duty. Singularly free from selfish and conflicting motives, he was at peace with himself. I sensed an inner quiet, rooted in a faith and hope that never failed him.

Earl had been critically ill for six weeks. He was much weaker, and the doctor, concluding that there was no longer hope for his recovery, thought the family should be notified. Sumner and his wife arrived the next day and so did Mary Alden with her family. At his first sight of Sumner all that Earl could say was "Sumner! Sumner!" over and over again.

Sumner was so overcome that he could not speak. He stood at the bedside and clasped his father's hand.

Looking up to him, Earl said, "It is late."

Three days passed. Early on the morning of August 22, Earl had a choking spell but after that showed no sign of discomfort. He appeared to be resting. In the morning the doctor arrived calling out as he entered the room, "How are you this morning?"

"Pretty good." Earl's voice, faint and weak though it was, had a distinct note of cheer.

The doctor made his examination, gave instructions to Clarence the nurse and completed his call in about fifteen minutes. After we left the room he indicated to me that Earl's time was short. He picked up his hat and was about to leave when we heard footsteps hurrying down the hall. It was Clarence. He appeared in the doorway and beckoned the doctor to come back quickly.

[1] Matthew 5:41.

In those few moments the end had come. Released from the frail and weary body, the valiant spirit that was Earl Covey had at last Gone Home. In November of that year he would have been seventy-six years old.

The Chapel service for Earl was as simple and beautiful as he would have wished. One of his last requests was that his former pastor, the Reverend Frank Reed, be asked to officiate. From his many years of acquaintance with Earl, Frank Reed paid tribute to him as "a good neighbor, a true friend and a highly skilled workman who dedicated that skill to the service of God and his fellow men."

The friends who attended the service gathered on the lawn afterward and were there when the family came out, following the casket as it was borne from the Chapel. They waited and saw us start on our way to the Forest Hills cemetery in Utica the place of burial.

At the family lot near the crest of the hill, the final words of committal were spoken, and the service was over. Before turning to go we paused for one last look. All we could see were flowers touched by the sunlight of the late afternoon.

That, too, was as Earl would have wished.

A Woodsman's Prayer

by Earl W. Covey

Dear Lord:

Just let me live my life as I've begun,
And give me work that is open to the sky and sun;
Make me a partner of the winds that blow,
And I won't ask for life that's soft and low.

Make me as big as the woods I roam,
As honest as the day is long,
Clean as the winds that blow behind the rain,
And free as the deer that scurries down the lane.

Just keep an eye on all that's said and done,
And right me sometimes when I've turned aside;
Guide me on that long, dim trail ahead,
Which reaches upward toward the great divide.

                                        Amen.

Inscription on the plaque on the distinctive great boulder beside the entrance to the former Twitchell Lake Inn. (The same boulder can be seen in the family photograph on page 29.)

**In Memory of
Earl W. Covey**

1876-1952

**A master builder, who lived so much in
tune with the life of nature,
that he was able to duplicate and enhance its beauty
in the creation of beautiful buildings
from Adirondack trees and rocks.**

Appendix

Tributes to Earl Covey

University of Florida
Gainesville, Florida

Mrs. Frances Alden Covey
By-Brook
Big Moose, New York

September 24, 1952

Dear Mrs. Covey:

Your good letter of recent date advising me of Mr. Covey's passing on August 22 brought me deep sorrow but also a profound gratitude that I was privileged to know him over the years. I am so grateful that you and he came by to see us, and I regret exceedingly that we could not return your visit before Mr. Covey passed on to his reward.

It is difficult for me to think of his absence from us. Somehow, he has seemed to have the same kind of immortality as the mountains which he loved. Deep down in our hearts, we knew that this was not true, and we had been prone to think of that kind of physical immortality rather than the kind of spiritual immortality which he really had. The former establishes his memory among thousands in this world who knew him so well, but his life gave him an even greater immortality in the realm to which he has gone.

Mrs. Miller joins me in sending to you our deep sympathy and understanding. We hope so much that you will come by to see us if you continue your yearly visit to Florida. Under any circumstances you would always be welcome. We shall be moving around

Christmas-time into a new home, which the University is building for us. It will be one of the most beautiful residences in the South, and you will always have an invitation to share it with us.

With every good wish, I am

>Cordially yours,
>J. Hillis Miller
>President

>Drew University
>Madison, New Jersey
>Office of the President

Mrs. Earl Covey
Big Moose, New York

September 18, 1954

Dear Frances,
 In looking through my files I discover I do have notes on the remarks that I made at the Memorial Service last year. I had already spoken of the five others who had passed away in the preceding year and in coming to the name of Earl Covey, I remarked:
 "What can one say? Here is a man who left a profound impression on the entire community and on each person connected with it. He is a man one can never forget - this quiet little person who was unafraid, unafraid of dangers and of death. How vividly I recall the experiences he once related to me in which he came face to face with wolves and bears, the former in Canada and the latter right here in the Big Moose area. Experiences that would frighten other persons only brought forth the greatest courage from him, and he faced them with a poise that always made him the victor.
 "Was that not the spirit with which he regarded the tragedy which came upon him in this church when the first Chapel was burned on the eve of its dedication? This would have thrown the

average person into despair but not Earl Covey. It sent him about his task all over again and with a determination to do the very best that he could to replace the original beauty, which he had built into this lovely woodland sanctuary. This was also the way he faced death. There was no fighting against it. There was no reason to struggle against it because he was a man of complete faith, a simple faith and a natural faith, nothing studied about it.

"May I give my own personal testimony that Earl Covey was one of the most genuine men I have ever met. I cherish a colored photograph that shows him shaking hands with the summer minister at the entrance of this chapel, but I cherish even more the memory of a man who will live with me through all the remaining years. I have testified already as to the impression he has left here. I would go a step further and say that Earl Covey, the man and his work, will prove an abiding blessing to this entire community."

These are about the words that I used at the service. There are so many other things I could say about him, and yet the effort to recapture his personality in full will always be unsuccessful because he was a man of such unique proportions.

I am sure that Big Moose is very beautiful in its fall foliage. Winifred joins me in sending very best wishes to you.

      Sincerely yours,
      Fred G. Holloway

From the Reverend Frank A. Reed, as officiating minister at the service for Earl Covey at Big Moose Chapel, August 25, 1952.

"Mr. Covey never led great congregations in worship, but he provided a place of beauty where they might worship in spirit and truth. He never preached to great congregations, but he provided the pulpit where others might proclaim divine truth. Clergymen who have shared in the ministry of the church agree that his was the more eloquent contribution."

Afterward

Earl Covey was my father. Frances (Alden) Covey was his second wife and my mother. My father died on August 22, 1952. In three months he would have been 76. By any measure he lived a remarkable life in an extraordinary time.

With little in the way of formal education, Earl became a quiet but popular craftsman, guide, builder, innkeeper, husband, father and community leader. His buildings were admired throughout the region of Big Moose, New York and as far away as eastern Quebec and the Gulf-coast of Florida. Writing in "Fine Homebuilding Magazine" in June 1987, John E. Barrows refers to Earl's many residential buildings, the stone bridge he built as memorial to his son William and the inns on Twitchell and Big Moose Lakes. Barrows describes Earl as "among the most prolific builders in the Adirondack style," and his work ethic as beyond reproach.

In the years between Earl's first breath in Glenfield, New York and his last sunset beside Big Moose Lake in the Adirondacks, human life saw revolutionary shifts in technology. The telephone, a practical electric light bulb, automobiles powered by internal combustion engines, radios, airplanes, frozen foods and the television were the subjects of fantasy at the time of Earl's birth in 1876. Any one of those advances in technology would have had an impact on those in the Adirondacks, but together, the broad spectrum of change altered the pace, scale and pattern of human life in ways that no one could have imagined in the 19th century.

There is no evidence that Earl was afraid of technology or change, but the ground that he loved and the life that he appreciated

Afterward

most were undisturbed by the modern era. I don't remember him ever talking about it, but he must have found great comfort in knowing that the place he called home was part of the Adirondack State Park. The Park was established in 1892, and the vast area including and surrounding Big Moose Lake totals more than 6 million acres, nearly the size of the entire state of Vermont. The Park is the largest publicly protected area in the contiguous United States, greater in size than Yellowstone, Everglades, Glacier and Grand Canyon National Parks combined.

Adirondack Park villages and communities (like Big Moose) include land that is privately owned, sparsely developed and protected. The state-owned land totals 2.7 million acres including that designated as "wilderness" and constitutionally protected to remain forever wild and that which is designated as "wild forest" and managed under slightly less restrictive land use controls. The Park, including the entire range of the high Adirondack Mountains, 3,000 lakes and 30,000 miles of streams and lakes, is a model of successful land use planning and land use management where people and natural areas coexist.

I am convinced that if Earl Covey had articulated his own hope for those who followed, coexistence between people and nature would have been his vision.

Earl was predeceased by his parents Henry and Emma (Chase) Covey and by his brother, Clarence. He was also predeceased by his first wife, of 25 years, Addie (Butts); two sons William and Henry and an infant daughter Elizabeth. Earl was survived by two daughters Emma and Mildred and his son Sumner and their families. His second wife, Frances (Alden), and I, Mary Alden (Covey) Williams, and my family also survived him.

My mother, Frances, was born in Centerville, South Dakota to Hannibal and Helen (Dodson) Alden. The Aldens relocated to Stafford Springs, Connecticut, and from there Frances attended and graduated from the Northfield School for Girls and Wellesley College in Massachusetts. As a college graduate and a continuing student of choral music and voice lessons, Frances made an unlikely prospect for settling down with the widowed innkeeper in Big Moose, New York. Nonetheless, the young Miss Alden fascinated

Earl, and he intrigued her.

Earl and Frances were married in Stafford Springs in April 1923. At the time of the wedding, he was 46. She was 33. Earl's surviving children from his first marriage were Emma (who was 26), Mildred (23) and Sumner (22). In a remarkable testament to mutual understanding, flexibility and love, Earl and Frances enjoyed a married life together characterized by compatibility and mutual respect for more than 29 years.

Frances provided companionship for the man who started out filling in for his father as an innkeeper and guide and emerged from a snow cave to build the Inn at Twitchell Lake. Two years after the sad loss of his first wife, Addie, Earl welcomed Frances as his office clerk, bookkeeper, confidant and second wife. Following their marriage, Frances adopted the remote beauty of the Adirondacks as her own home, and she devoted herself to understanding and appreciating the Covey vision.

After Earl's death, Frances spent one more winter in Florida and then established her winter home in Utica. She was committed to perpetuating Earl Covey's memory. As a faithful member of the Big Moose community and trustee of the Big Moose Community Chapel, she did that with grace and skill. The story of their life together cannot possibly be better told than through her words in the pages before mine in this book.

The Earl Covey Story was originally published in 1964 while Frances was still living at ByBrook, the house that Earl built beside the outlet at Big Moose Lake. Frances sold ByBrook in 1973, but she retained life use of it, and she spent every summer there until the last few years of her life. She died in Wolfboro, New Hampshire on March 25, 1989. In three months she would have been 100.

Hillis Miller, the first summer minister at the Big Moose Community Chapel and Earl's close friend even in Florida, died in 1953. During his tenure as summer pastor at the Chapel, Hillis was a psychology instructor at the College of William and Mary and Bucknell University. From 1935 to 1941 he was President of Keuka College. In 1941 he was appointed associate commissioner of education for the State of New York, and in 1947 he was named president of the University of Florida.

Afterward

Following World War II the University of Florida experienced a huge surge in enrollment, and under Hillis Miller's leadership it became a coeducational university and enjoyed an era of massive expansion of facilities. Expansion at the University included the first medical school in Florida. In 1953, complications from rheumatic fever as a teenager caught up with Hillis, and he died in November 1953. He was 54.

Hillis Miller's wife, Nell, continued to work for many years at the J. Hillis Miller Science Center, named in honor of her late husband. After supporting herself and continuing on as a popular member of the University of Florida community she died in 1993. Two sons, including J. Hillis Miller Jr. survived her.

The original Camp Crag was built by Henry Covey in 1880. By 1888 it was the first permanent Covey home at Big Moose Lake. It was there that young Earl discovered his aptitude for multiple skills as he worked beside his father as a cook, host, builder and guide. Under Henry's management Camp Crag maintained a distinctive personality in which his affluent and carefully selected clientele enjoyed a beautiful setting inaccessible by road. Camp Crag offered privacy and quiet. By 1922 Big Moose Lake had developed from wilderness into a popular vacation spot, but Henry and his second wife, Margaret Rose, were unable to maintain Camp Crag. The property was sold to Edward Morse, a wealthy businessman from Brooklyn. Morse died in 1930, and although the main Camp Crag lodge had burned the property was sold to a land speculator. Some of the original outlying camps remain to this day, converted into elaborate and highly desirable summer homes in the area known as Crag Point Road.

At the Twitchell Lake Inn many original features are substantially undisturbed. The distinctive palisade style walls with logs stood on end remain as do the lovely interior paneling and the now-dated plumbing and knob and tube wiring. After Earl Covey moved his family to Covewood, the Inn at Twitchell Lake was operated seasonally for many years and continued to provide a lakeside sanctuary for visiting families. Eventually the inn was closed, the cabins were sold and the main building became a private home. In July 2009, an auction of the Twitchell Lake Inn property attracted enormous interest among those who recalled its heyday. The successful high bidder was from Blue Mountain Lake and a family with considerable experience in the hospitality industry. Hope that the building will be returned to its place of prominence among Adirondack inns is widespread.

Covewood was sold in 1951 to Claude Vernon "Major" Bowes, a Utica native who spent summers in the Adirondacks, and his wife. The Bowes continue to operate the property as a simple rustic resort from May through October. Families, some in their third generation, return to Covewood year after year for the peace promised by Big Moose Lake. There are no televisions and no phones. Covewood's kitchen is quiet now, and guests bring their own food and linens to apartments in the Great Camp-style main house or one of 18 cottages. The stone fireplaces, huge interior timbers and the vertical slab siding are unchanged and much the same as they were when first set in place by Earl Covey in the 1920's.

Many, including Earl Covey himself, considered the Big Moose Community Chapel his crowning achievement. The Chapel is beautiful for its wood- and stonework, much of which was created by Earl's own hands, but its continuing attraction to those who are familiar with it has taken on a life of its own. Sixty years after it's construction the Chapel is still a popular place of fellowship and nondenominational prayer. Every Sunday through the summer, year-round residents join summer residents in an outpouring of faith in their community. Typically there are two services in which standing room is the only space available. There is an active Sunday School program and regular organ recitals, choral evenings, the guides' dinner and "balsam bees" in which volunteers make balsam pillows as an annual fundraiser are all well attended.

As much of organized religion in America is hoping for a renewed commitment from its parishioners and struggling for new and younger members to join them, the appeal of the Big Moose Community Chapel remains vibrant and strong. The number of multigenerational families that would not think of any other place for a family wedding or funeral is enormous. For thousands of people, who have stood in the shadows of the Big Moose Community Chapel, there is no other place quite like it - anywhere.

Ida (Ainsworth) Winter is a lifelong resident of Big Moose. She served for 38-years as a trustee of the Chapel holding every office on the board and is well known is its historian and year round guardian. Ida says, "The Chapel is a treasure for all those privileged to visit the building or attend its services. It stands today as proud and sturdy as it did at the time of its dedication. It continues to be the focal point of summer activities at Big Moose." Ida was christened and married in the Chapel. All of her children were married there as well. She smiles as she remembers being a part of the square dancing led by Earl and Frances Covey. "He was here at the right time of his life," she says, "and it turns out that he had a huge part in shaping what this area still is today."

Another longtime friend of the Covey family is Barbara Kinne Wheeler. Barbara came with us to Florida and went to school with me one winter in Clearwater. She is still fond of saying that "Frances was like a second mother." Barbara describes Earl as "a genius."

Jean Brownell Dena is one of Mildred Covey Brownell's children. Still a summer resident at Twitchell Lake, Jean compares her grandfather Earl Covey to those almost mythological individuals whose influence resonates in their communities - in some cases - forever. "The summer congregation at the Chapel numbers in the thousands. Generations of camp families live many miles away, but they cherish the chance to return and gather together as families on those summer days inside the Big Moose Chapel."

Rev. Dr. Richard McCaughey has been the pastor of the Chapel since 1999. Rev. McCaughey cites Earl Covey's lasting influence on the area through his buildings, which continue to be must sees on architectural tours in the area. "But," he says, "there is a subtler, yet just as important, lasting influence from Earl Covey's character and leadership. In an era that tended to separate people as locals or summer residents Earl Covey stood out as a reference point all by himself - respected, admired and [apparently] listened to by everyone. While the division between locals and summer people still persists in a way, Earl Covey bridged the divide with a grace and wisdom that is still felt today.

"Nowhere is that inclusiveness more evident than in the life of the Big Moose Community Chapel. The Chapel is an inclusive community of faith - spiritually, denominationally and socially." Rev.

McCaughey says, "To this day, leadership in the Chapel is not determined by socioeconomic status or geography but by spiritual gifts, graces and commitment. As to fellowship, the Chapel is at the center of much of the social life at Big Moose, not only by means of its own activities but also in the relationships that develop as people take part in those activities in or away from the Adirondacks."

Barbara Sayer is from one of the many summer families that return to Big Moose each year for, as she says, "rest and re-creation." It is through the Chapel that Barbara finds, even as an outsider, a genuine sense of belonging. She describes Earl Covey this way: "His lasting influence is his authenticity. His buildings reflect the sense of permanence of the mountains and the wonder of Creation. To see the Chapel, Covewood and the memorial bridge over the outlet of Twitchell Lake is to see into the builder's soul. He was a reverent man who cherished the rocks, the woods and the waters of the Adirondacks. His way of life seems to have derived from his philosophy of simplicity and endurance."

Like many who have bowed their heads in personal prayer in the Big Moose Community Chapel, Barbara likes to cite the Woodsman's Prayer, which appears on a bronze plaque on the Chapel wall. It was written by my father, Earl Covey. "Make me as big as the woods that I roam, honest as the day is long, clean as the winds that blow behind the rain, and as free as the deer that scurries down the lane."

Last summer, in 2009, the Memorial Woods were opened on a wooded hillside across the road from the Chapel. According to Rev. McCaughey, this is unique for a summer chapel. Dedicated in memory of one of the Chapel's founders The Rev. Dr. Percy Wightman, the Memorial Woods offers a columbarium for the inurnment of a loved one's ashes or the option of spreading ashes in the surrounding woods together with installation of a commemorative plaque. Memorial Woods is open to all those who are or were active in the Chapel and to anyone, and this is an increasing number, who considers the Big Moose region to be home, even if that presence is or was only seasonal.

As I think of my parents, I rejoice not only in their gift of life

Afterward

and love but also for the priceless gift of a wonderful childhood in a place of magnificent beauty and peace. My love of the lakes and mountains, my appreciation for the kindness and generosity of family and friends, the joys of square dancing and the satisfaction of a job well done come from my dad. The love of books and the determination to finish, that which was started, come from my mother.

For the strength and beauty my father expressed in wood and stone, which comfort and delight us all, and for my mother's skill and understanding in recording it, I am truly grateful. With the far-reaching branches of my extended Covey family including descendants of Emma, Mildred and Sumner, I salute the gift Earl provided to us all. To all who have contributed to this book and to those whose lives have somehow been enriched by an association with the Coveys I extend my hand and my own hope for continued enjoyment including long lasting fresh air and clean water at Big Moose.

> Mary Alden Covey Williams
> January 2010